M●RE
THAN A
NUMBER

THE POWER OF **EMPATHY** AND **PHILANTHROPY**
IN DRIVING AD AGENCY PERFORMANCE

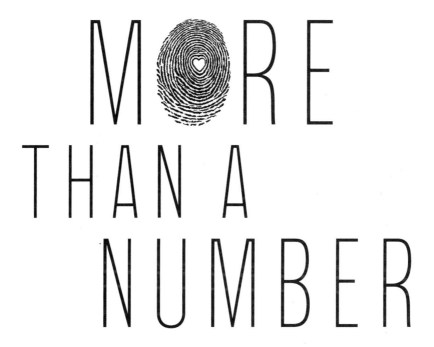

MORE
THAN A
NUMBER

ED MITZEN

ForbesBooks

Published by ForbesBooks, Charleston, South Carolina.
Member of Advantage Media Group.

ForbesBooks is a registered trademark, and the ForbesBooks colophon is a trademark of Forbes Media, LLC.

Printed in the United States of America.

10 9 8 7 6 5 4 3 2 1

ISBN: 978-1-94663-379-8
LCCN: 2019919785

Cover design by Carly Blake.
Layout design by Jennifer Witzke.

This publication is designed to provide accurate and authoritative information in regard to the subject matter covered. It is sold with the understanding that the publisher is not engaged in rendering legal, accounting, or other professional services. If legal advice or other expert assistance is required, the services of a competent professional person should be sought.

Advantage Media Group is proud to be a part of the Tree Neutral® program. Tree Neutral offsets the number of trees consumed in the production and printing of this book by taking proactive steps such as planting trees in direct proportion to the number of trees used to print books. To learn more about Tree Neutral, please visit **www.treeneutral.com**.

Since 1917, the Forbes mission has remained constant. Global Champions of Entrepreneurial Capitalism. ForbesBooks exists to further that aim by bringing the Stories, Passion, and Knowledge of top thought leaders to the forefront. ForbesBooks brings you The Best in Business. To be considered for publication, please visit **www.forbesbooks.com**.

To my late father, Ed Mitzen, who made me cry at the dinner table when I was ten years old, teaching me a valuable life lesson I never forgot.

CONTENTS

THE PITCH

The first time I was involved in a real advertising pitch, I was a client getting pitched. It was years before I ever started an ad agency, when I was a marketing manager tasked with selecting an advertising agency to launch a new medication for asthma.

We had five agencies come in and present to us. I remember sitting in our conference room, full of nervous energy. See, I didn't know how to make an ad, and I hoped I would be able to evaluate the agencies by how effective they could be at driving results for my brand. After all, success in my role as a marketing manager relied on the performance of the agency I selected to launch this product.

At the time, I was unaware that the traditional pitch process I was about to undergo was flawed and would not meaningfully help me vet potential agencies' performance capabilities for my brand. I didn't realize how little the pitches would actually show me about the internal culture of my new agency partner or how important its culture would be to drive its performance, and ultimately, my brand's success.

The first agency arrived in a parade of suits and ties. The people introduced themselves, each with a seemingly loftier title than the last. I remember wondering, How are there so many vice presidents at this company? Who will actually work on my account? Whom should I pay attention to?

While an outsider may expect a pitch from an advertising agency to be entertaining (especially if they have watched the popular TV show *Mad Men*), any marketing leader knows that agency pitches are more often death by PowerPoint.

That's how that first pitch went. Eighty-something slides rushed through in ninety minutes. The next pitch was very similar. Power suits. PowerPoint slides. Vice presidents.

The third, the same. Of course, there were subtle differences. Some agencies mounted boards around the room and turned them around like Vanna White on *Wheel of Fortune* to reveal their creative mock-ups. Some had paper handouts, some had disks with more information, but it was all variations of the same process.

Every agency started with its background. Then the team would cover the same issues: Here's what you asked us to present. This is our research. Here are our strategic takeaways. This is where we recommend positioning the product. Here are four or five creative examples of how we could roll this out to your customers and a tactical plan that summarizes how we'll be in market. At that point, they were usually running out of time and turning hastily to "Thank you; do you have any questions?"

I remember wondering, *What should I be looking for? Am I choosing the best presenters? Or who has the best strategy? Am I trying to see which creative sample I like the most, even though we haven't been involved in any of the creative discussions yet?* I had no sense of the heartbeat of any of the agencies, and truth be told, I didn't know how important their internal culture, or lack thereof, would be to my success.

At the end of the day, I made a decision based on—I hate to say it—the people I liked most in the room and who I felt had the best mock-up creative work. In hindsight, now that I've worked as a marketing director and founded two successful advertising agencies over the past twenty years, I will tell you that I've never been part of a pitch where the creative presented in the pitch actually went to market.

I've also realized just how ineffective the traditional pitch process is. Isn't it bizarre that you meet a few groups of people for two hours each, one after the other, after which you're supposed to decide who you will trust to launch your product and work side by side with you for the next several years?

More often than not, because most marketing executives simply don't know what truly drives performance in advertising agencies, the pitch process turns into a two-hour personality contest played out over creative and strategy presentations. Often you haven't worked with these agencies before, so in a way, you're getting married with a contract before you even date. After all, what can you get from a two-hour pitch besides charisma and some inkling of an agency's strategic and creative thought process?

Wouldn't a better process give you real insight into the big questions that can make or break your success with a firm, such as, What are their people like to work with? Will they be true partners and challenge us or just do whatever we ask them? A year from now, will the people in the room still be involved with my business or even working at the same agency? Are they ethical, hard-working people I want to be in the foxhole with?

At the time of my first pitch, I wasn't aware of all that could change once I signed. I simply assumed I was choosing the people I'd be working with for the next three or four years. I didn't realize that the internal culture of the agency was hidden from me, and the people presenting to me didn't accurately reflect what it was like to work with that agency. I wasn't aware that the charismatic creative director in a room full of vice presidents was due for a promotion and would be off my account in three months and onto bigger fish. I didn't know the account director who shook my hand at the start of the deal was already looking to jump ship to another agency because the work environment was so toxic.

At the time, I was focused only on what I thought mattered: the creative and strategy in the pitch and the personalities and reputations of the presenters.

I've since moved over to the other side of the table by starting my own ad agencies and running them for many years, and I've learned so much that can help marketing directors be better informed than I was about how to evaluate and manage their ad agencies.

A PROVEN WAY TO EVALUATE AND MANAGE AD AGENCY PERFORMANCE

I'm writing this book to help marketing directors pull back the curtain on agency culture, so that they can drive positive performance to produce great work sustainably for years to come.

Over the last twenty years, I've successfully built two advertising companies that have grossed over $500 million in combined revenue as a result of a positive culture with a foundation of respect, empathy, and giving back.

All the lessons I will share in the coming pages rest on this foundation: a positive culture is the key to driving performance and growth. A positive culture must have its roots in empathy. I don't just mean empathy for your customers, which is clearly a prerequisite for successful advertising. I mean empathy to your employees and to your communities, which in turn creates an internal culture that powers performance.

The culture I've built at Fingerpaint has earned us an extremely high rating on Glassdoor compared to most of our competitors. We grow 30–40 percent year after year, with happy employees and happy customers. But of all the numbers that measure the impact of the agencies I've founded, I'm most proud of this one: in more than twenty years as a CEO in an industry notorious for layoffs and staff turnover, I have never laid off a single person.

> **In more than twenty years as a CEO in an industry notorious for layoffs and staff turnover, I have never laid off a single person.**

Here's the thing—even after this many years running ad agencies, I still don't know how to make an ad. I don't know how to use InDesign and Photoshop. I'm not a creative genius or strategic maestro. Our staff actually teases me about it. But I absolutely know how to find the best people and how to treat them so that they will be happy and create great work for our company, for one another, and for our clients.

If you read on, I will share with you a proven way to select an ad agency and to manage the relationship effectively. I will take you behind the curtain to reveal why the usual approach that most businesses take to selecting and managing their agencies is not optimal and how evaluating and supporting a proper culture is the key to business success.

If you're a marketing director and you spend millions of dollars a year with agencies, but you don't really understand how they work internally and don't feel like you're in a position to drive the best work from them, then read on, and I'll show you how they operate and how you can enable your team for success so that you accomplish what you set out to do with your agency partner.

If you work in advertising or own your own shop and feel like the culture needs big improvement, I'll show you ways you can take it to new heights. By improving your culture to be more inclusive, collaborative, and positive, your creative work will also soar.

After reading this book, you'll know what to expect when you walk into the conference room to meet the various agencies pitching you. You won't wonder what is important, as I did once upon a time. You'll know how to select and nurture a partner that will produce great work for you for years to come. You don't have to be an ad person to get great work from your ad agency. I'm the perfect example of that.

Of course, choosing an agency with an empathetic, productive culture is just the beginning of a successful partnership. Once you've chosen the agency, I will show you how to foster a productive working relationship with it that leads to great work. By using the lessons in this book to align yourself with a positive ad agency culture, you'll be well on your way to driving performance and growth for your brand.

CHAPTER ONE

WHY IS IT SO DIFFICULT TO SELECT AN AD AGENCY?

"We've always done it this way." That's the reasoning behind the approach most marketing departments use to evaluate ad agencies. It's also the most dangerous phrase in business. "We've always done it this way" has proven to be the Achilles heel of many established industry titans that fell to younger, more innovative companies. It's led to enormous losses of money, time, and opportunities in the marketing and advertising world, as companies have followed a pitch process that simply does not give them the tools to effectively evaluate their crucial advertising partners.

While some companies have attempted to improve it, there's a fundamental issue in the heart of the current pitch process: it doesn't enable clients to learn the culture of each agency, to understand how the agency works, or to truly get to know who will actually work on their account.

Most marketing directors have no idea what makes a good agency and a bad one, and agencies currently win business in a truly archaic fashion. Clients give agencies a creative assignment, and agencies present how they would strategically solve the problem.

Typically, clients will have one or two marketing executives oversee a pitch, and they will provide each potential agency with a detailed overview of the market. They'll share market research and strategic plans and host phone calls with the agencies to answer questions ahead of the pitch.

Very rarely will clients provide a budget ahead of time. It's bizarre because you'd expect they'd say, "We have $5 million to spend; show us how you would spend it," and then evaluate the teams based on their use of the available funds. Instead, they want to protect those numbers, so there's often a cat-mouse game that's played, where they'll say, "Tell us what *you* think it will cost to do the job."

This is problematic, of course, because an agency can build a plan for a variety of budgets. Think of it like buying a car—you can buy a Ford or a Ferrari, depending on budget. But without the budget, it's a guessing game: Should an agency present the blueprint for a Ferrari to a client, when they may only have the budget for a Ford? Or should they build a Ford and present it to someone expecting a Ferrari? Either way, expectations will not be met.

There's a very cookie-cutter approach to the pitches. Most clients expect case studies, an overview of research, a strategic review, four to five creative concepts, and a full tactical plan with pricing and a timeline. For all that, they generally allot two hours to each agency. With all that content to cover, it's difficult to dive deep on any single subject and impossible to thoroughly examine an agency.

To try to get a sense of the agency and who will work on their account, clients usually send a list of rules for the pitch for agencies to follow, such as these:

- Only people who will be part of the core working team are allowed to attend.

- Each agency is allowed no more than six people.

- Present the company background, history, and accolades.

- Give a brief overview of services and capabilities.

- Provide management and key personnel bios.

- Show examples of previous work.

- Create new positioning statement and core messages.

- Present four creative campaigns.

- Provide a top-line tactical plan that will be executed according to proposed strategies and detail budgets.

These prompts create an expectation that clients will evaluate agencies based on sample creative and strategy, the talent of the agency people in the room, and the agency's overall reputation.

Given that prompt, agencies have two hours in a conference room to present. Most clients will stack these appointments back to back, so they can meet four to six agencies over a couple of days. The current process really only provides insight into what each agency has done for past clients, its experience in a category, and a glimpse of how it thinks creatively.

Usually, after the pitches, companies will call references or have an online reference submission, which means we at the agency reach out to our references to have them populate a form online. Let's face it: agency references are just like the references you put on a resume—they're good friends who will say how great you are. It may not be your three top customers or the most relevant customers to the client. The reference check, like the rest of the pitch process, has a fundamental problem: no matter what prompts you give or what specs you ask for in a creative demonstration, you can't get a sense for the heartbeat of an agency through a two-hour presentation.

KEY ISSUES

There are two key issues with the current pitch process:

1. Companies do not spend enough time deeply getting to know the agency's people.

2. The metrics companies use to evaluate agencies are not effective.

Two hours is simply not enough to vet an agency. While asking for very specific things to streamline that process may seem to help, it doesn't actually work. Here's what happens on the agency side for each pitch:

One person quarterbacks each pitch and chooses the team to bring to the pitch. The pitch itself is practically theater. At a two-hour presentation, agencies know that winning or losing is as much about if the client likes the people presenting as it is about capabilities. The pitch doesn't give any insight into the heartbeat of the agency, into what it values, and into the team members who will ultimately work on the project.

The strategy and the creative presented is important, but sadly, a lot of times pitches simply become personality contests. This happens because the pitch window is short, and the creative is often pretty similar. There's this sea of sameness that rises from the cookie-cutter approach to agency selection.

The other thing agencies do to try to win business is highlight past work in a pitch—even if it's from another department. For instance, a large global agency's consumer department created the iconic green slimy Mucinex mascot. For years its health-care team presented it to clients as an example of the agency's health-care work—even though it was created by a completely separate business unit. The client doesn't know that a different division of the company created that work, so they may expect that the people they're hiring will be the creatives who worked on that assignment, which is not the case. It's very common for global agencies to use campaigns they've created for consumer brands as samples for their health-care teams, even though the teams do not work together.

Even creative work done specifically for the pitch is not a true test of the crucial abilities an agency needs: to be able to solve a problem in collaboration with the client. All the agencies start without the client's deep knowledge of what does and doesn't work for the product and create their pitches in a vacuum, with no input from the client, so it doesn't simulate how you will actually work together in the future.

Sample creative done without client collaboration is not a good indicator of future success.

No matter how you slice it, sample creative done without client collaboration is not a good indicator of future success. As a result, many companies choose their agency based on the people in the room. If they're duds or not polished, they can have the best ideas in the world and get overlooked.

Knowing this, agencies bring their best presenters to the pitch. Most of the time, clients ask for six people to present. Usually, agencies bring two senior creative people, who oversee every brand in the company. They approved the creative materials in the pitch and can present them well, but they weren't the ones in the trenches doing a lot of the thinking. The head of the agency, like myself, will also usually be present for a pitch but will not be involved in the day-to-day strategic and creative discussions for the client. Agencies also usually include a strategy executive, who monitors multiple clients. Finally, two midlevel account people, who will be the day-to-day contacts for the client, join the presentation.

As a client, you can *ask* for only presenters who will be allocated mostly to your business, but it's simply not realistic. If an agency is running properly, it doesn't have six talented people sitting around waiting for your business to come along. If it did, it would mean the agency either just got fired from another account or the company is not good at managing its resources.

The other problem with asking to meet *your* team in a pitch is that it takes time to build out the appropriate team for each project. The strategy of what will be done on your account and the timeline of when it will be done still has to be defined before a team can be assembled for the project.

Let's say the first year of a project is strategy and creative concept development. That means that you may not see the web development team for another year, so they won't be allocated to your business at the time of the pitch, but they will absolutely be critical to the agency's success or failure on your account, which means you should evaluate them before choosing a partner.

From an agency perspective, it also needs its best presenters to win business, and there is no actual contract holding the agency to use those presenters on any particular client's business. So, if an agency has great presenters that can think on their feet when questions come up, the agency will bring them to every pitch—but it can't have them work on every account.

The pitch process simply does not do a good job of connecting the client with the people who will actually work on the account. Approximately twenty-five people will contribute to a $5 million account—you can't meet them all in a two-hour pitch, especially if you limit attendance to six people. As a result, in a traditional pitch, clients never see the art directors and copywriters who will drive the performance of their brand. There are very talented people behind the scenes—writers, editors, graphic designers, digital developers, media strategists, and project managers who aren't department heads in a pitch but who are absolutely critical to the execution of the strategies.

Success or failure for a client comes down to the other twenty people who aren't in the pitch. How talented are they? Are they happy? Are they motivated? Are they ethical? Are they good listeners? Do they think the agency is a good place to work? Is there a lot of turnover?

When I was a marketing director, I didn't realize how much of my success with that agency would be tied to people I did not meet at the pitch, and most marketing directors today don't either, because they've never worked in an ad agency. They choose the best people in the room. The problem is, six months down the road, the team often gets swapped out, so the people you met are no longer working on your business, which is very common. Or some key people from the pitch leave the company, and you're left holding the bag.

Unfortunately, losing key members of your team happens too often in the ad business, because it's a hard-driving industry plagued with high turnover. The other thing that often happens is culture clashes between agencies and clients. Let's say you're a collaborative client and want to bat around ideas with a creative team. If you hire an agency that expects you to tell it what you want so the agency can deliver it, the partnership will not be successful.

EVALUATE EACH AGENCY'S CULTURE

Here's the key to avoid hiring the wrong agency: *you need to evaluate the culture of the agency—not just the presentation skills of six people.* You don't sign a contract with the people in the room. You choose an agency, so you need to have confidence in the culture of that company to deliver for you, regardless of who is in the room the day of the pitch.

If you find an agency that has a strong company culture, you can trust that it will always have good people to work on your business. Its culture is a far more telling indicator of future performance than the creative talents and presentation skills of six people in a conference room—even if those six people were to work on your account.

> If you find an agency that has a strong company culture, you can trust that it will always have good people to work on your business.

There is more to choosing an agency than evaluating creative. Most marketing departments lack an understanding of the importance of the human capital of the agencies and the importance of culture.

In chapters two and three, I'll provide in-depth strategies and tools to help you evaluate an agency's culture, but as a preview, one proven method is for marketing executives to conduct a full-day working session on site at a prospective agency with their extended team. Solving a problem together gives you a much better sense of the important things at an agency, such as, Is there good chemistry among the team? How does our team work with them? Do they get along? What's the turnover of the extended group? What is the culture like? Is it a healthy company? Will they walk through fire for each other and their clients, or are people just punching a clock because they need the money, waiting to jump ship as soon as they can find something better? You can sense the energy of the agency in a very tangible way by working with the people at their home base.

We held a pitch recently during which a potential client came and spent two days with us in Saratoga Springs, New York. They visited our creative ideation space, which is down the street from our regular office, and brainstormed with us on how to launch their brand to the consumer market place. They immersed themselves in our process, met all the extended team members, and gained an understanding of how we think. It gave us an opportunity to provide feedback to them and for them to provide it to us to test a working relationship.

That company put in the time required to vet each agency it considered working with, and it made an informed decision as a result. Not to brag, but yes, the company did choose to trust us with its business.

Spending more time evaluating each agency provides a far more telling picture of future success than the theater that often takes place in two-hour pitches, in which decisions are often based on an artificial relationship with strong presenters that will not be working day to day on your business. In a two-hour pitch, you are in fact grading a show, not an agency.

Instead of comparing presenting groups, you should spend time investigating the culture of the agency, because the agency's internal culture will ultimately determine how successful the partnership is. There are many varied company cultures in the advertising industry. However, many agencies have similar bureaucracies, largely stemming from one common principle: profit over people.

THE MISGUIDED PRINCIPLE OF THE AD INDUSTRY: PROFIT OVER PEOPLE

Whether by ignorance or dumb luck, I started an ad agency having never worked for one. I didn't have any preconceived notions about hierarchies or how the culture "should" be. As such, I was spared from the most dangerous words in any business, which are the words that open this chapter: *"We've always done it this way."*

I simply applied the approach of how I wanted to treat people to my entry into the advertising world in hopes that everything would work out. As I interfaced with more and more people in the ad business, I learned that the inside workings of an ad agency, the people you choose to hire and the way you treat them, and the way you operate in your communities directly affects the quality of your work and the relationships you build with clients. If you hire good, empathetic people who want to make the world a better place, and you can empower them to do so, they will create great work for you that will ultimately lead to sustained success.

Unfortunately, for many agencies, financial profit is the guiding principle, and that leads to many practices that run counter to producing great work, such as the following:

- When an agency needs to hit a profit number, it cuts senior staff and has the junior people take on the business to save money.

- Agencies often limit raises to 2 percent to meet corporate earnings projections and try to soothe employees with non-sensical title bumps in lieu of better pay and perks.

- Agencies routinely lay off entire teams when it loses a client, which destroys the morale of those remaining.

Common practices like these plague the advertising industry. Luckily for me, I didn't know any of these when I started my business, so I built my business without them.

A lot of the big advertising firms make every decision based around profit and numbers and earnings. They think in terms of, "We can't invest in training because our margins will drop," or "We have to hire more junior people because that's where we make the money," or "We can't have a company-wide community service day because that'll cost us too much in lost billable time."

I contend that they're looking at it backward. Creative agencies need the people to be inspired, which is impossible when the top motivator driving leadership's decisions is financial impact. That doesn't inspire

Creative agencies need the people to be inspired, which is impossible when the top motivator driving leadership's decisions is financial impact.

people. Companies will make more money if they support and enable their most valuable commodity, which is their people.

Building a positive culture of collaboration; treating people with respect; and having an appreciation for your staff, their families, and those less fortunate in the areas where you work will ultimately make for a better business, both in profitability and quality of work delivered to the client.

I'm sure Jack Welch would scoff and say I'm a weak leader because I believe in culture, and I don't fire the bottom 10 percent every year, or rule by fear, or institute archaic hierarchies in which senior-level people beat down on junior-level people.

But I don't believe in those methods. I don't believe in burning people out, replacing them fresh young ones whom you don't have to pay much, and starting the cycle over again. I feel that it takes strength to lead with empathy and to care for your staff as more than simply financial assets. As a result of this empathetic culture, we've been able to avoid many of the problems that plague most ad agencies and irritate clients, such as an apathetic staff and high turnover.

WHY DO AD AGENCIES HAVE SO MUCH TURNOVER?

One of the things you notice as a client when you work with typical ad agencies is that they're incredibly bureaucratic. Everybody has a big inflated title, and you have no idea what they all mean. There will be a copywriter, senior copywriter, group copy supervisor, and creative director of copy. As a client, you don't know who is who, but everybody you meet seems like a big deal.

The title system within the agency world works very similarly to the banking industry's title system. It's ego driven and layered with bureaucracy that I think is counterproductive to doing great work.

The problem with agency bureaucracy is that there are too many cooks in the kitchen. There may be four people working on copy, which creates waste and unnecessary revisions—and every hour costs you money. The art director who works closest to the client has more knowledge than the senior executive, but the senior executive feels like they have to weigh in because they're "the boss." Often this ends up marginalizing the lower-ranked individual, whose creativity is vital to the success of the campaigns.

This bureaucracy also hurts agency employees, who don't get proper recognition and pay for their work. You don't have people truly empowered and responsible for the work with so much overlap.

As a result, agencies soothe their employees with title bumps every eighteen months in the hopes that they'll stay with the company. Let's say someone is hired as an account coordinator. Eighteen months later, they move up to senior account coordinator—but there's no real difference in what they're doing. Then they become an account executive. Then a senior account executive—which is the same job but with a fancier title. However, this system doesn't really work, because at a certain point, the titles stop making the employees feel warm and fuzzy when they're not backed up with significant increases in pay, perks, responsibilities, and learning opportunities.

That's why there's so much turnover in the agency world. People have to jump from company to company to earn more pay and responsibility. If they stay in one place, they get stuck in the bureaucratic ladder that is designed to keep them motivated but not provide real career growth.

We structured Fingerpaint differently, because I didn't come from the ad agency world. We don't have titles, and we don't have offices. Our culture is very collaborative. Everybody is out on the floor working together. I never wanted a twenty-four-year-old to be afraid to speak up in a meeting because they weren't a vice president or they hadn't been at the company long enough. We're all in this together, and we provide growth opportunities based on talent, not bureaucracy.

CULTURE DRIVES PERFORMANCE AND GROWTH

If you're considering hiring an ad agency, you need to evaluate more than its creative and strategy. If it has high turnover or a reputation on Glassdoor for being a rough place to work, then it won't consistently deliver effective work because it will lose its great people. It won't be able to provide continuity and a relationship of mutual growth to you if it uses and abuses its people. The harmful effects of a negative culture may not show up at first, but ultimately they will lead to the work product breaking down.

If a company doesn't care for its employees, eventually they will burn out. Then new people will come in and need to learn your business all over again, wasting time, effort, and, of course, billable hours, which could have been prevented with some simple in-house empathy.

If the agency is consistently losing good employees, it doesn't really matter if you meet the team on your account in the pitch—they may not even be there by the end of the year.

At the end of the day, the ad business is a people business. Every time I look back at when we've gained business, when we've lost business, when clients have been happy or upset, it all comes back to a simple question: are we taking care of the folks who are working on the account?

I have seen so many companies that don't take care of their people fail. We put our flag in the sand and say: we put *our* people first and our clients second. In the end, it leads to better results for all of us. We take care of our people, and they take care of the clients.

That's the value of a good company culture, and in the next chapter, I'll share what you should look for when selecting an agency and how you can gain a competitive advantage by more effectively evaluating agencies.

CHAPTER TWO

WHAT TO LOOK FOR WHEN SELECTING AN AGENCY

Agencies are all about people. There are no machines, widgets, or products that the business is built around. When you select an agency, you are investing your company's money and trust into a group of human beings. When I chose to start Fingerpaint, my entire mission was centered around caring for people. In summer 2009, that mission was tested when I got a phone call that threatened to end my business. Luckily, the way our company rose to the occasion transformed that threat into a challenge that galvanized our company around a people-first culture.

Fingerpaint was born in April 2008, in the heart of the economic downturn. Even though it was a tough business climate, we managed to find a few clients. A year later, we had fifteen employees, and the future looked bright. I had been able to create a company based on a culture of empathy and caring for my employees.

Then my phone rang.

I was in a hospital waiting room while my wife underwent a medical procedure when I took the call. It was our largest client, and he was calling to cancel his contract. The client had just received an unfavorable ruling from the FDA and therefore was suspending all sales and marketing efforts—effective immediately.

I remember sitting in that hospital in a panic. We just lost our biggest client—two-thirds of our business—with one phone call, due to no fault of our own. The economy was in the tank. Ten of our fifteen employees were working on this brand, and I had their salaries on the books.

"Oh my God. What are we gonna do? How much longer can I go on?" Questions rang through my head like an air-raid siren as I pulled out my computer and feverishly poured over my finances, calculating how long I could put salaries on credit cards to cover my people. I cared deeply about my employees and was determined to keep them on, but I couldn't see a way to do it. It felt like an overwhelming blow.

In that moment, I understood the harsh conditions that have turned the advertising industry so cruel. Traditionally, when ad agencies lose a big client, they lay off the team working on the account. We had just taken a hit that would knock any other fifteen-person ad agency out of business.

After hours of reflection, a new emotion emerged, overcame the math, and took hold of me: defiance.

"You know what? Screw it. I'm not letting anyone go. I'll call everyone I know and scrap together enough business to tread water to keep my people on, and we'll be a stronger company for it."

When I came into the office the next day and called a meeting with the whole company, many of my employees thought they were about to lose their jobs. Everyone who had worked in an agency before had seen their best friends or themselves shown the door because a client significantly reduced or eliminated its budget.

Grief filled the office like a fog. I got everybody together in our conference room and cleared the air: "We're not letting any of you go." The room was still—frozen by disbelief.

I continued, "I will need you to work on projects that aren't in your sweet spot, and we have to work together. I'm gonna pull projects in that have tight timelines. It won't be the most glamorous work, but we're gonna save everybody's job and weather this together until we can restore everything."

I didn't realize at the time the long-term effect that choice would have, grounding our company culture around making sure that we're not all about profit and we won't cut people whenever a client goes away. But from that moment forward, a rallying call grew within our company: *Ed doesn't lay people off.*

The ensuing months were the most challenging I've faced in my entire career. To survive, I liquidated everything I had. I maxed out three credit cards to cover payroll. I sold my car to pay for office furniture. I took a second mortgage on one of my properties to pull out equity. At one point, I was about two or three weeks away from being insolvent.

When I had sold my previous company, I bought my mom a modest house in upstate New York. Now, faced with insolvency, I had to take a $100,000 home equity loan on that house so I could keep the company going. That was a kick in the teeth for me. But I believed in our group, and I was determined to keep us going.

I never told anybody just how much I'd leveraged myself to support Fingerpaint, but when it was the darkest, I remember thinking on a Wednesday, "I don't know how I'm going to make payroll on Friday."

I was fortunate that I had a local bank in town that worked with me through the dark times and did some things for me that a major bank wouldn't have done, because the people who worked there knew me personally.

People teased me that I kept going to the bank all the time. They didn't know I was there to try to figure out how to make payroll for the following week. They never saw me stress about it or project fear.

From a leadership standpoint, I knew I had to be the voice of encouragement and optimism. There were days I just wanted to curl up into a ball and give in, but I knew I had to keep that to myself and cheer everyone on, let them know that we'd get through this, and make the phone calls to pull in work so that we could dog-paddle until things turned around.

I still remember our team's first big win to pull us out of the tailspin. We had an opportunity to pitch to some people we had worked with in the past who were based in St. Louis.

All our great people whom I had kept on board rallied together and brought their A game to prepare for this pitch—we probably did more work than necessary, because we didn't have a lot else to do, and everybody knew that our backs were against the wall.

We brought a large group to St. Louis for the pitch to show the client that they were our priority. We even offered to lease a small office in St. Louis and staff it with a couple of people if they wanted a local agency presence. They didn't take us up on that, but they were so impressed by our team and our commitment to them that they chose us for their business.

Little did they know that win gave us the fuel we needed to not crash and burn and gave me the spirit to carry on. I'll never forget those first Fingerpaint employees who came through when I needed them, and I would do anything for them down the line.

Fast-forward ten years, and we've grown from 15 people to more than 350, but the rallying call is still true—I've never laid anyone off. There's a mystique around our company related to it. At industry functions and in trade circles, we're discussed in curious whispers as "the agency that's never laid anybody off."

That commitment I made to our employees has helped us enormously across all areas of the business. Our best people grow with us over time, getting better at what they do and building meaningful relationships with each other and our clients. They take on more responsibility and build an institutional knowledge that is unique to us. Our reputation of caring for our employees helps our recruiting too. The best creatives in the country come work with us precisely because we value them as people and invest in their continual success. All of this leads to big dividends for Fingerpaint—when we talk to our clients, our ability to attract and retain the best people is one of our biggest selling points. Our people are our agency, and I value them above all.

THE PEOPLE ARE THE MOST IMPORTANT PART OF AN AGENCY

When you are choosing an agency to work on your business, you are not choosing a campaign or a commercial—you are choosing a collection of people to support you. People are the most essential part of an ad agency. Roughly 80 percent of an ad agency's expenses are human costs—payroll, benefits, and so on. There are no technical or material assets that even come close to matching the value of the people at the agency. The quality of the work rises and falls based on the talent at the agency.

In this chapter, I will share with you a high-level view of how you should spend your time and resources to successfully evaluate the culture of each agency that you consider hiring.

INVEST TIME IN SELECTING AN AGENCY: YOU'RE ALREADY INVESTING MONEY

The first thing you need to change from the traditional pitch process is to spend more time evaluating each agency. Simply put, it takes more than a request for proposal (RFP) and a two-hour meeting in a conference room to evaluate an ad agency.

Your agency contract may cost you millions of dollars directly, and it is intended to bring in even more money in revenue for your business. In the health-care space, common multiyear contracts can be between $5 million and $10 million a year, so you're looking at a $25 million to $50 million long-term cost.

Even a smaller size deal is still an enormous investment. Recently, we won a pitch for a company that produces syringes for diabetes care. If we perform well, it will spend $2 million a year with us for the next five or six years, which in our industry is on the smaller side of deal sizes. That means for this "small" deal, the company has chosen to invest $10 million with us, not to mention trusting us to help it grow as a business.

While many health-care shops consider that a small account, $10 million is still a lot of money where I come from. Because these investments are so large, it's important that you invest your time doing your due diligence before choosing an agency so that you can find the right partner.

When you think about that dollar amount and the short window most companies spend choosing an agency, it seems crazy. Further, if you think about the longevity of the working relationship, choosing a team you'll work with for years is very important and deserves time and attention. You don't want to have to change the team out early because it isn't working, so make sure to get to know them beforehand.

Choosing a team you'll work with for years is very important and deserves time and attention.

Other than the sales force, one could argue that no other relationship is as important as the advertising team you assemble to work on your account. It's important to see the actual teams to understand the quality of the people and to see how empowered they are to do their jobs. Is your money going to good use? Or are you being charged to feed a bureaucracy where everyone has to sign off, leading to bloat and ineffectiveness?

A thirty-page RFP submission and a two-hour presentation is simply not enough information to determine such an important investment of your money, time, and trust. So once you've taken RFPs from companies, narrow your choices down to your top four or five finalists and prepare to spend a significant amount of time evaluating each of them.

HOLD PITCHES AT THE AGENCIES

You should visit each agency that you consider hiring at its location. Very few companies actually visit the agencies' offices for pitches, but there are enormous advantages to doing so. You begin to get a sense of an agency's culture from the moment you arrive. It's similar to buying a house. Pulling up to the curb can reveal more than a Zillow listing photo ever could. Each house you walk into has a certain feel.

One may be contemporary, another may look like a log cabin, and another can have an antique charm. Similarly, each agency will have a vibe particular to it.

There are so many data points that convey culture that you can't discern a reliable sense of culture by asking an agency in your conference room to express its culture. But we as humans are naturally very attuned to the environment around us, and just by visiting the agency, you are able to more fully evaluate the company. There's so much information that comes to you through all your senses being at the agency that you will never get in your office. Your eyes, ears, and mind all process data so you can get a read on culture very quickly. You will learn more about the company by touring its space than you could ever discover from a traditional pitch meeting at your office.

In your own conference room, you can try to find out if employees are happy by asking the pitch team how long people stay at the company or to tell you the agency's core values. But any answer they provide will pale in comparison to actually seeing the agency teams working, hearing the back-and-forth between the team members, and watching the creativity happen.

As you're walking through the agency, you don't even need to ask questions—you will simply see—does the office environment seem like it's conducive to collaborative work, or does it feel drab and cold? Do the people seem stressed out or happy? Is there a good vibe in the office? The environment really matters when you're concerned with producing creative work.

Visiting the agency will also pull you out of your day-to-day distractions and put you in the right frame of mind to be present in the evaluating process. Your team members aren't knocking on the conference room window asking for a few minutes of your time. You're not getting text messages and emails or being pulled into meetings. You're more focused and dialed in to the task at hand: finding the right partner for you.

Perhaps the greatest advantage of visiting a company's location is that you will get a realistic preview of the level of care and service you can expect to receive. Did the agency set up welcome signs for you that show they value you? Did they reserve parking spots for you to make it easier for you to attend the meeting? Have they considered dietary restrictions for lunches and planned accommodations for you? Have they given you a tour of the office? There are many little touches that will tell you if the agency is staffed with caring, attentive people who will value you and treat you well or if you're just another business meeting to them.

SPEND A FULL DAY WITH EACH AGENCY

On top of visiting the agencies in person, plan to spend more time than most companies traditionally do to vet each one. Plan to use your RFP submission to select four or five finalists and then spend a day with each agency so you can fully vet them all in a week's time.

We've already discussed the significant financial investment you're going to make in an agency and its importance to your success. From where I sit, choosing such a crucial partner warrants a week of due diligence.

Spending a full day at each agency gives you the ability to vet the agencies in multiple ways, such as hearing presentations that are more in depth on important topics and having a back-and-forth discussion about your strategic challenges to assess how they think. Conduct an impromptu workshop with the agency, in which you raise a certain market challenge, and give the agency an hour to huddle and brainstorm solutions and then come to you and present ideas. This gives you an opportunity to see how the employees think on their feet and how they work together.

While at the agency, take time to meet the extended team: the project managers, the writers, the art directors, the web designers, and so on. By doing so, you can get a sense of the types of people the agency has employed who will make or break your product launch or campaign. You can get to know them over breakfast and lunch and find out if they're the type of people whom you want to be in a foxhole with. Having dinner with the team is a great way to immerse yourself in the group and see how bonded the team is, how invested they are in their company, and by extension, how invested they will be in your brand should you choose to work with them.

When you are selecting an agency, look for one that empowers its people to succeed.

Often, a company will have to hire additional staff to fulfill the needs of your business, so seeing the type of people who work there currently, and how happy those people are, sheds light on who the agency will be able to hire and retain in the future. Is the team diverse? Are they a mix of junior or senior people? Where is the company bringing talent from? Is it having trouble recruiting people?

Meeting the team also shows you how the agency's business is set up to support you: Is the digital web team in the office or in another country? Is the company offshoring app development work? What percent of its staff is freelance? Has it invested in quality people, and does it train them and develop them, or does it simply farm out your account work to a rotating cast of freelancers it can hire cheaply?

While you are there, ask the agency leadership to introduce you to other key players at the company and demonstrate how they work together to serve a client, so you can understand if its process is efficient or if it has many approval layers that will cost you more money and slow down the work.

As you meet everyone, pay attention to and ask about the following: What is their approach to client service? How often will you meet with your account team? What is the tenure of the people on the team? Are they all fresh faced and not going to be there very long? How big are the teams? Is the creative director managing twenty-five creative people, which means they won't be day to day on any account? Or are teams smaller and more directly connected to clients?

You can discover all of this and more if you make the time investment to truly understand the people behind the sign on the door.

HIRE UP

I believe when you are in the position to hire people or contract a team, you should aim to hire people smarter than you and give them freedom to do what you hired them to do: let them be smart and creatively solve challenges. When you are selecting an agency, look for one that empowers its people to succeed.

Some agencies are good at hiring up, and others fail at it, largely because of their leaders. A lot of agencies fail because the agency CEOs clamp down on the talent around them as opposed to trying to help people improve. Many agency presidents have climbed through the ranks of agencies, so they've been either former creative directors or heads of accounts, and they feel that because they've risen to the top, then they have to be the smartest person in the room. They have to be the best at picking the creative. They have to be the best at driving the strategy for the client. What tends to happen is that attitude marginalizes the people below them, leading to poor work and unhappy employees.

It's easy to spot this type of leader in a pitch. If an agency president dominates the pitch, even though you know they won't be working day to day on your business, beware. They do this because they are used to being the ringleader, so they feel that they have to run the show, and it's a good indicator that they're not hiring smart people and letting them work. Creativity thrives in an encouraging environment, so even if you see good creative work in the pitch, if one of these leaders is at the helm, they are not giving their talented people the freedom to create. Smart, creative people will tolerate being marginalized for only so long and eventually will search for a more fulfilling role, leaving you with an agency that doesn't suit your needs.

The core function of my role as founder of Fingerpaint is to hire smart people and support them. Because I didn't grow up through the agency ranks, I always rely very heavily on the people I surround myself with. As I've gotten more and more involved in this business and my company has grown to more than $60 million in annual revenue, I see every day how beneficial it is that I've hired people who are infinitely better than me in many areas.

If I give myself credit for anything, it's that I am comfortable not being the smartest person in the room. I recently hired someone to start our office in New Jersey who had previously been running a larger agency than Fingerpaint. In the first part of the year, he and his team had already won $9 million in business and hired thirty-five good people. I could never have done that so quickly.

I see my connection to my people as a support function: I am here to give them what they need to do their jobs effectively. If they have questions on budgets, or if they need somebody to kick around ideas with or consider who they want to hire, I'm there for support. They work for me, but I look at it as I work for them. I ask them to tell me what they need or what sticking points they're facing, and it's my job to essentially be the general manager and make sure that everyone is empowered to do their jobs.

I had lunch with the new head of our New Jersey office recently. I asked him what he needed, and he said they were having some challenges with our health plan because it was designed for the New York office, and he'd had some trouble getting information he needed from our HR department.

That's something I could take back and, without being heavy handed, ensure that everyone had what they needed so they could focus on doing their amazing work. That's my role as founder—to support the amazing people at my company, not to dominate pitches or tout my expertise. Clients need to see the people actually doing the work for them, and my job is to support and empower them.

ONE OF MY ALL-TIME FAVORITE PITCHES

I've always believed in showing our customers how much we value the real people at our company who do great work for them. Years ago, we pitched GlaxoSmithKline for a $10 million annual assignment. We were a small agency without much brand recognition, which meant we had to decisively win the pitch; if we tied with a larger competing agency, we'd lose.

While we didn't have the brand name of some larger agencies, I knew we had amazing people. I believed that if the client saw our people, they would understand our unique value. So I took the whole agency to the pitch meeting at the client's office. While our presenting group was inside the conference room, our entire company stood outside the office waving signs and showing support for our team and the customer. To this day, the head of agency relations at Glaxo-SmithKline tells me it's the best pitch he's ever seen.

I didn't bring the whole team as a stunt. I brought everyone to the pitch because I felt that while only a few of us could be in the room, all those people were ultimately the ones who would be working for GlaxoSmithKline. I felt the client needed to see them, and after that pitch, its team certainly agreed. We won the business.

Because I'm on the agency side, I was able to introduce the team to the client in such a way that it could truly see our company and understand the type of people we had within our ranks, but most agencies will not do so. To successfully vet the agencies, you have to take matters into your own hands and go out to visit the agencies, meet the teams, and immerse yourself in their cultures.

In the next chapter, I'll share a practical score sheet that you can use when conducting agency pitches to help you ask the right questions and effectively evaluate the aspects of each agency that will accurately indicate its ability to produce great work for you.

CHAPTER THREE

THE SCORE SHEET: A PRACTICAL GUIDE TO VETTING AGENCIES

Once, my team and I pitched to a client with twenty people on the marketing team. We were competing with another agency whose owner was the best friend of the client team's senior marketer. During the pitch process, all twenty of the client's team members rated both agencies on a score sheet. When it came time to make a decision, its senior marketer felt that his friend's agency was the clear choice. However, the team summed up all their score sheets, and their leader was surprised to find that we had significantly outscored the competitor. The company chose to work with us, and its marketing team was excited because they knew the decision was made based on which agency met their needs—not because of a personal relationship.

Having a consistent score sheet to grade each pitch is a great way for your team to anonymously rate agencies and fairly compare one against each other, which helps you more objectively measure each agency's strengths and weaknesses.

I've included a score sheet in this book that you can use while evaluating agency pitches to help you ask the right questions and score agencies according to key metrics, so you can remove the swings in emotion from the evaluation process and compare agencies on metrics that matter.

This score sheet is not intended to be treated as a gospel or to turn pitches into interrogations—don't feel the need to ask every question or rate every category. It is intended to be a road map to help you organize your thoughts and keep track of what you should consider while receiving pitches.

While many of these questions may look familiar to a traditional pitch process, pay particular attention to the culture section, as I've added some questions that few companies ask but that can help you get a sense of each agency's culture.

In the pages that follow the score sheet, I'll share the thoughts behind each section to clarify why that section is important and to provide more context on the goal behind certain questions, so that you can know what to look for when using the score sheet to grade pitches.

RFP EVALUATION–AGENCY CAPABILITIES PRESENTATION

Date:

Evaluator Name:

Company Name:

Please evaluate the agency based on each of the following criteria on a scale of 1 (lowest) to 10 (highest):

Approach: 1 2 3 4 5 6 7 8 9 10

1. Is the approach fresh and/or unique in some way? — YES | NO

2. Did they describe how they monitor/measure performance? — YES | NO

3. Did they adequately demonstrate their use of digital, innovative, and differentiating capabilities? — YES | NO

4. Did their recommendations and approach for the business make you want to use them? — YES | NO

5. Did they demonstrate the difference between their approach in each unique market against traditional programs within your industry? — YES | NO

6. Did their creative proposals display strategic thinking? — YES | NO

7. Did the agency engage in healthy debate with you? — YES | NO

Experience: 1 2 3 4 5 6 7 8 9 10

1. Did the agency describe its background and expertise? — YES | NO

2. Did it seem to you that they understood your requirements? — YES | NO

3. Did they demonstrate relevant experience and/or analytical capabilities? — YES | NO

4. Did they adequately explain how they activated and engaged consumer audiences to take action? — YES | NO

5. Did they effectively describe the issues or challenges they faced, the movement in the market they created, and what action(s) they drove? — YES | NO

6. Did they demonstrate the ability to test and measure impact using innovative approaches to consumer marketing in an evolving landscape? — YES | NO

7. Are there any conflicts of interest with existing accounts of theirs? — YES | NO

8. How many clients have they had for longer than four years? — _____

9. On average, how long do employees stay with the company? — _____

10. Who worked on the case studies they presented? — _____

Culture: 1   2   3   4   5   6   7   8   9   10

1. Did the agency describe its mission and culture?   YES | NO
2. Did the agency's people convey enthusiasm, energy, and positivity?   YES | NO
3. Were they commercially minded and not just creative or artistic?   YES | NO
4. Did they ask the right questions on the right subjects?   YES | NO
5. Did the style of the company seem compatible with your needs?   YES | NO
6. Do you want to work with this agency for the next several years?   YES | NO
7. Did the agency assemble the right people or team for this opportunity?   YES | NO
8. Is this agency aligned with your messages (do they get it)?   YES | NO
9. Are they philanthropic and ethical?   YES | NO
10. Are they passionate about any causes?   YES | NO
11. Are their values aligned with your organization's?   YES | NO
12. Does their leadership care about your business?   YES | NO

Value: 1   2   3   4   5   6   7   8   9   10

1. Are you getting bang for the buck?   YES | NO
2. Does the proposal fit within current budgetary constraints?   YES | NO
3. Is there any confusion over the budgets? (If yes, provide details.)   YES | NO

Any further comments:

Next, I'll provide some background on each section of the score sheet and dive deeper into selected questions to shed light on their importance and what to look for when you ask them.

SECTION 1: APPROACH

This section is meant to help you evaluate how the agency approaches creative challenges. Healthy debate is something that is underused but is vital to your success.

An agency full of yay-sayers will not deliver great results for you. Some agencies will say yes to anything, especially during a pitch, to make you feel good and win your business. Does it always defer to you? Tell you all your ideas are great? If so, it's likely just saying what it thinks you want to hear to win your business and will never challenge you in a productive way.

On the other hand, an agency that claims to have all the answers is not productive either. Several agencies have a reputation for being pompous and posturing—"It's our way or the highway." They feel that they have to be the smartest people in the room. It's easy to fall for it, because they project so much confidence in pitches, but eventually, that act wears thin—especially when they cannot execute, and those agencies are often replaced early on as they fail to collaborate well.

The happy medium is healthy debate. There are agencies that can challenge assumptions and work with you to find the best solution. When selecting an agency, it's important to find one that will help you improve ideas and be collaborative. Healthy debate doesn't mean "do it my way." It means

An agency full of yay-sayers will not deliver great results for you.

questioning, reasoning, and trying to discern the core objective: "Have you thought about this? Have you tried this?"

During pitches, you can pick up on which type of agency you're dealing with by paying attention to how an agency responds to your statements. Does it simply agree with you all the time? Do the people disagree strongly and make declarative statements to assert their knowledge? Or do they ask you for more insight and challenge your assumptions to find out more? The third one represents an ability and willingness by an agency to engage in constructive conversation.

For example, if you tell an agency you want a six-wave virtual reality campaign, it might say, "OK, great," or "Eight waves are more effective, so that's what you should do." These are examples of yay-sayers or know-it-alls, respectively. Or the team members can ask, "How did you arrive at six waves?" That's a sign you're meeting with an agency that can engage in healthy debate to find the best route forward.

A good agency will ask you exploratory questions and engage in a brainstorming session with you, rather than simply touting its knowledge or acquiescing to all your ideas. Of course, as we've covered, to actually evaluate its ability to collaborate, you need to spend enough time with the agency to encourage healthy debate.

VETTING CREATIVE CAMPAIGNS

Creative campaigns should *not* be the most important factor influencing which agency you choose. They are often created without any meaningful input from you or any market testing and will *never* actually go straight to market. However, while the visuals aren't a great indicator of what an agency will do for you in the future, creative concepts are a great way to explore how an agency's team thinks.

The concept should deliver on a strategic point. Visuals can (and will) always be changed, but the work should strategically meet a goal. Ideally, you should collaborate with the agencies before the pitch ever occurs to create a prompt that provides both sides with a clear sense of the strategic goal, which includes the following:

1. The current perception in the market

2. The perception the company would like to change that to

3. The key market drivers

4. The brand personality

5. The brand's positioning

6. Key tonal factors to consider

If an agency can deliver a strong message that checks those boxes, it's a good indicator that it can tackle creative challenges.

Most people put too much stock in the creative concepts, especially on the "wow factor" that can come from a stunning visual—even one that misses the strategic point. The problem with choosing based on an impressive visual is that those pitches are created simply to wow you—without respect to actually succeeding in the market. When they go through development, and market testing comes into play, most people lose comfort with that new look and are left with a creative team that hasn't hit the mark strategically, so they revert to redoing the same thing everyone else is doing. Why do you think every health-care ad on television looks so similar?

That's why most hospital logos are blue. When focus groups test logos, doctors are comfortable with blue. It doesn't mean that you couldn't have a very effective green hospital logo, but doctors are generally uncomfortable with it. So an agency may show you a logo or design with a color palette you've never seen before in a pitch, and you'll be excited by the originality, but when you test it later on and realize it doesn't fit your market, you want to be sure that there is strategic soundness behind the visuals that exists beyond being fresh and new in the pitch.

When you're looking at sample creative work, ask yourself, Could I see this in the market? Is it relevant? Is it strategically sound? Is it clever? Will it break through? Is this different than what's typically seen? But keep in mind that all this creative work was done before any meaningful market testing and has much less bearing on the success of the agency than the other factors on the score sheet.

SECTION 2: EXPERIENCE

The purpose behind this section is to help you evaluate the relevance of an agency's experience to your particular business. Successfully evaluating an agency's experience involves gaining an understanding of the experience of the people you will work with directly, rather than the agency's brand overall.

An agency's background is a very important indicator of success, but it's very easy to confuse experience and relevant background with simple name recognition. There are of course the major agencies that have been in business for half a century, such as Saatchi & Saatchi and Ogilvy. You may know their names, but the name represents a company employing more than twenty thousand employees across many business units and multiple continents. The names don't provide any insight into the team directly working on your account and the quality of work they'll do for you.

So how can you dig deeper than name recognition? Research the companies' market-specific stature: In your category, are they known as a hot shop? Have they been tied to successful launches in the past?

Are the brands they are responsible for outperforming the competition? Are they winning awards for their creative work? Are people clamoring to work there?

You can find information about awards online and ask for examples of their successful launches in an RFP. For some other indicators of their performance, you'll have to ask the agency's team during the pitch. For example, to find out if people really want to work there, you can ask: How many people apply to work there each year? How many leave each year? Is the senior leadership turning over? How many layoffs has the company had in the past few years? Most agencies have layoffs periodically, but multiple recent layoffs indicate a poorly run business or that the company is losing accounts. If that's the case, you should ask yourself, Why are they losing accounts?

SCORE SHEET QUESTION: Did They Demonstrate Relevant Experience and/or Analytical Capabilities?

When evaluating an agency's experience in your market, it's important to take a step back and gauge the importance of direct market experience. Experience within a category is very important for certain markets, while in others, a quality creative team with strong analytical capabilities may offer a fresh perspective in your market, which can have more value than specialized experience.

If you're working with a challenging product involving a steep learning curve, such as a drug for multiple myeloma, finding an agency with deep oncology experience will be crucial. However, if you're in a space that requires less specialized knowledge, it can actually benefit you to search for a firm that hasn't done a ton of work there, so you don't end up rehashing the same ideas that have been used in the past.

For example, allergy drugs are not particularly complicated, so if you are launching a new product in the allergy market, you may find more value in a fresh perspective from a team that hasn't worked extensively in that space and whose members can learn the market quickly and offer something new.

So rather than looking for the "allergy experts" who have exhausted all their best ideas in that category, you can look for a team who has a history of successful launches and phenomenal creative campaigns in other markets, who can likely replicate that success for you in your market.

At the end of the day, you're trying to evaluate the talent in the room, so if you know your product requires specialized experience, ask about it and value it accordingly. If your product doesn't, then don't place a premium on experience in that market—look for how people think strategically and creatively and trust that they can apply their skill sets to your market.

SCORE SHEET QUESTIONS: How Many Clients Do They Have Longer Than Four Years? How Long Do Employees Stay with the Company on Average?

It's important to see how long people stay with each agency—both clients and employees. The industry average contract length is about four years. If an agency you're meeting with has many contracts end after two years, that shows something is not working.

Sometimes there's a perfectly good reason why an account may end early, especially in the health-care field. The company may stop promoting a product because it goes off patent. The company could get bought by a larger company that wants its existing agency to take over. There are certainly valid reasons for a shorter-term relationship with some clients, but that should be the exception, not the rule. Ask agencies, How many clients do you have that are over four years? If they have a stable base of long-term business, it indicates that their clients are happy with them.

The same concept applies to employee turnover. How long are their employees there on average? If employees are quitting after one or two years, that's a sign of instability that will affect the quality of the work they provide for you.

SCORE SHEET QUESTION: Do Executives Hire the Agency If They Move to a Different Company?

Oftentimes marketing directors change jobs; do they bring their agencies with them? If so, that's a great sign that the relationship is top notch. If not, it shows that the agency is not delivering well enough for people to trust it again. Ask agencies how many executives have hired their agencies on behalf of multiple companies.

SCORE SHEET QUESTION: Who Worked on the Case Studies Presented?

Case studies are a great indicator of performance but *only* if they are case studies for the actual team that will work on your account. When presented with a case study, be sure to ask who worked on it. And of course, if you have a traditional pitch in your office, don't expect the people who worked on that case study to be in the room. Odds are they're back at the agency's office producing more great work.

SECTION 3: CULTURE

Culture is the most critical aspect for you to evaluate. An agency's culture will be the leading indicator of how it will perform for you. Are the employees enthusiastic and passionate? By visiting an agency, you can see how much the people care—are they just cashing a paycheck, or are they really invested in the success of their clients?

This section of the score sheet provides you with a series of questions that can help you evaluate a company's commitment to culture. I will share more details about the tenets of good company culture in chapter four. For now, I'll briefly touch on some of the questions in the score sheet to add some context so you can more deeply understand what to look for when using the score sheet.

SCORE SHEET QUESTION: Are They Commercially Minded or Do They Just Want to Win Awards?

Commercial focus is a big deal, and surprisingly, it is often over-looked. At the end of the day, agencies need to help you sell product or change behavior, but some creative teams become so focused on creating award-winning work that they lose sight of the fact that it's not their primary goal. They forget that their ad needs to quickly convey a message to a doctor or drive consumer behavior. Instead, they aim to look clever and do something unique.

This is very common in the insurance market and in Super Bowl or other prime time commercials; each ad tries to be funnier than the next, but at the end of the day, are they driving business? You often see hilarious ads that are essentially very clever short films, but you don't know what they're advertising. If no one remembers who the ads are for, and none offers a value proposition to the customer, then what's the point?

It's very easy to be impressed by brilliant creative work even if it doesn't directly convey your value proposition, so it's important to pay attention to the priorities of the creative team. When you're meeting with agencies, try to uncover whether they are commercially minded. A great way to assess this is to evaluate what questions they ask. Are they looking to understand and address your core business challenge, or are they simply focusing on creating attention-grabbing material?

SCORE SHEET QUESTION: Did They Assemble the Right Team for This Pitch?

As I've mentioned before, the people you meet in a pitch will not necessarily work on your business, but score this based on if the agency brought people from each department to give you a clear understanding of who will be responsible for each aspect of your business. To get a true reflection of your agency team, hold the pitch at the agency.

SCORE SHEET QUESTION: Do You Want to Work with Them for the Next Several Years?

Trust your gut. All the score sheets in the world don't mean anything if you can't get excited about working with the agency's team. Would you like to have a beer or a coffee with this team? Will they be difficult to work with, or are they nice people who make your life easier? Will you enjoy spending hours with them behind the two-way mirror doing market research, or would you rather have a root canal than spend a prolonged period of time with them?

> All the score sheets in the world don't mean anything if you can't get excited about working with the agency's team.

SCORE SHEET QUESTION: Are They Philanthropic and Ethical?

Philanthropy is important because it influences the type of people who choose to work for the agency. Many creative people are not motivated by money or simply winning business for business's sake. They want to feel they're making a positive impact on the world. Therefore, a company with clear philanthropic initiatives, especially ones the employees directly care about, will be able to attract and retain excellent creative and ethical people.

During your evaluation process, try to uncover these issues: Do they have a larger purpose besides making money? Are they in the press for the right reasons? Are they giving back to their communities? Are they making the world a better place? Are they doing good pro bono work?

People want to know that they work for a company that's not all about money and that is truly trying to make a difference in the world. We have a dedicated person at Fingerpaint in charge of philanthropy and corporate giving, which is one of the founding principles I wanted to instill in my company.

All our employees see that we actively work to make the world a better place, and it makes them feel great. Employees come to us to see if we'll support charity efforts with organizations that are important to them, and 99 percent of the time, we will. Some of these efforts are small, like running a 5K to support a cause or taking a polar plunge, and some are larger and more personal.

We recently got involved with the Concussion Legacy Foundation, which helps with chronic traumatic encephalopathy (CTE) and concussion injuries from sports. The father of one of our writers died from CTE. Before coming to Fingerpaint, she worked for another agency, and she wanted to donate time and get her employer involved in helping support this organization. Her former agency declined because it saw philanthropy only as a pathway to win awards and receive good publicity and didn't see her cause as one that would help achieve this.

When she joined our company, she brought the proposal to us, and we said yes right away. She was amazed that there was no bureaucracy getting in the way and that we would support her because it was important to her. We assigned a creative team to create a television commercial inspired by scientific studies that revealed a shocking statistic: kids who play tackle football before the age of fourteen are more likely to end up with CTE than childhood smokers are to contract lung cancer later in life. Our commercial shows kids playing tackle football and then lighting cigarettes on the ride home to illustrate how serious the repercussions are for kids playing tackle football and to promote a safer alternative: Flag Before 14, which encourages kids to play flag football until their brains are fully developed.

We created that campaign because CTE is a health and wellness issue and because it's important to a member of our team. She felt great seeing her team rally around her to help her with something this near and dear to her heart, and all of us benefited from that camaraderie.

Why is an agency's philanthropy important to you? Well, not only does it help an agency keep great people, but it also represents a company culture of doing the right thing and acting ethically.

Ethics can make or break your work in any market, especially in the health-care space. If we're asked to help educate doctors on a particular diabetes therapy, we will do so responsibly and not just try to sell pills or injections. If you're working on an oncology drug to treat breast cancer, you want to make sure that you communicate the message in a way that encourages appropriate use, rather than trying to get every patient on that program. Ensure that you choose an ethical agency partner who understands the importance of your product to patients and their families.

When you find an ethical philanthropic agency, you can be confident that it will care for you and do right by your team and your brand.

SECTION 4: VALUE

Of course, any partner you choose must fit into your budget. So it's a good idea to share your budget with your top choices before the pitch meeting and evaluate how they would allocate the funds.

More than that, you want to see if you're getting the bang for your buck, which you can see by visiting the agency and meeting the teams and then evaluating these issues: Is there bloat? Are there so many senior people that you can't really distinguish what each person does? Does it seem that the company empowers its teams and operates efficiently? If so, that will save you time and, of course, billable hours.

An agency's hourly rate is not always the best indicator of value. If one agency has a higher hourly rate but uses half as many billable hours to complete a project as another agency due to operational efficiency, it can certainly provide a better value.

Has each agency laid out a clear cost estimate that breaks down how it will allocate your budget, or is it unclear? You should have a good sense of where your money is going by the time you've finished meeting with the agency.

Did the agency clearly demonstrate the reason for each service that it included in its proposal? Many agencies pride themselves on a full-service approach, but I like to say at Fingerpaint that we provide a "right-service" approach because we look for which avenues best achieve a strategic goal, rather than trying to sell as much as possible.

As you consider the value of each agency, pay attention to each service offering it provides and the benefits and costs associated with each one to understand if you are getting the right bang for your buck.

In the next chapter, I'll dive into more detail about what a positive agency culture looks like, so you can more clearly see what to look for as you visit each agency.

CHAPTER FOUR

THE FOUNDATION OF A POSITIVE CULTURE: EMPATHY AND PHILANTHROPY

A positive culture rests on the foundation of empathy. My late father, who was my biggest role model and best friend, taught me the importance of empathy to a team's success when I was a youngster playing peewee football.

When I was in fourth grade, I desperately wanted to play Pop Warner football but was too young, and my father actually forged my birth certificate so I could play a year early, which made him Superman to me. Of course, this was well before anyone knew about CTE risks from playing tackle football. I was just so excited to play and grateful to my dad for letting me play, even after I got the snot kicked out of me because I was tiny.

The following year, I was the quarterback of the peewee football team. We were a group of sixty-five-pound kids trying to play tackle football. I had no idea how to lead people, but I tried my best to motivate the team, pounding on my linemen's shoulder pads and barking instructions. No matter how much I yelled or how hard I pushed our guys, defenders kept getting through our line and tackling me. And we kept losing.

I remember coming home one night frustrated and sat at the dining room table with my father. I didn't understand why my teammates weren't blocking for me. My father knew, and he told me. Bluntly. "You're yelling at your teammates, so they think you're a jerk. That's why they're not trying hard, and that's why you're getting sacked all the time—because these kids don't want to play for you."

That broke me. The weight of my actions flooded over me, and I sobbed at the dining room table. I could visualize myself grabbing my teammates by their shirts and shouting at them. I could see the hurt in their eyes. I was completely oblivious to the fact that I was damaging these kids whom I desperately wanted to lead.

From the next practice on, I was very conscious not to yell at anybody. I told them how great they were doing and made a concerted effort to encourage them and not to berate anybody. Lo and behold, our season started to turn around. We became a better team, and I built relationships with my teammates. That was the first time I learned that I needed to treat people better and that leadership requires caring, not force.

I built a business on the foundation of making our people the number-one priority.

My father's leadership lessons stick with me to this day, but too often, business leaders go about it as I did in peewee football—belittling their teams and trying to shout them into compliance. Little do they realize they and their clients get sacked by the repercussions day in and day out.

In the past few chapters, we've discussed the importance of positive culture, but what does a positive culture really mean? In this chapter, I'll outline the foundation of a positive culture and discuss how I've fostered a culture of empathy at Fingerpaint that drives performance for our business and our clients.

CULTURE IS EVERYTHING IN ADVERTISING

The internal culture at a company defines the work the company produces. Culture influences who chooses to work for you, how long they stay, and the quality of work they do.

The core of Fingerpaint's internal culture is empathy—empathy to employees, to customers, and to the communities that we live in and recruit from. Customers don't always realize the connection between a healthy agency culture and the work they're getting. They don't see that it's creatively inspiring people. It's producing better work. It's making sure that the people treat the clients the same way that they're used to being treated.

In this day and age, kindness and compassion are not common themes. I built a business on the foundation of making our people the number-one priority. That empathy is the secret to keeping the creative juices flowing year after year.

Advertising specifically requires a deep understanding of the people you are trying to reach. To create an emotional connection, you need to have empathy for what people feel. What they want. What they *need*. This is especially true for the industry where my company does the bulk of its work: health care.

To educate physicians on a drug for Alzheimer's, you need to understand what the caregivers are going through and what the newly diagnosed patients are feeling. You have to be able to connect with people so that they feel you understand what it means to walk in their shoes and that you care enough to help them get the best therapy that they can get.

Advertisements need to come from a place of empathy, and to create empathetic work consistently, advertisers need to work at a place with a culture of caring that allows them to work with empathy.

BUILDING A TEAM OF CARING PEOPLE

Business is a team sport. To have an empathetic culture, you need people who care for each other and work well together. There may be a six-person team building a very complex website. They will have different perspectives and different talents, but at the end of the day, everyone has to be a good team player for the project to work.

I made the decision a long time ago that I will not work with jerks. People who are super talented but can't get along with others tend to destroy the team dynamics, and the work product suffers. When people don't want to work with a difficult person, they don't include them in communications or work discussions. As a result, communication breaks down, projects aren't in sync, everyone is unhappy, and the team cannot win.

My job is to put the best team on the field that can get the work done. When I build teams, I look for people who lead with empathy. Of course, culture starts at the top, which means I have to show the entire staff that I care for them.

LEADING WITH SUPPORT, NOT FORCE

Culture starts at the top, and I've found that the best results come when leaders support their people and help them get the most out of life, rather than trying to squeeze them to work harder and harder. People can sacrifice for the job for only so long before they burn out.

It may sound counterintuitive, but sometimes prioritizing life over work actually improves the work product. I've found that once you hire good people, you don't have to push them with crazy deadlines to squeeze productivity out of them. In fact, the opposite is true: you need to encourage them to log out and care for themselves and their families so that they don't burn out.

When I look at what other agencies are doing, I see why they falter at building a positive culture. In typical agencies, there's an expectation that "you're going to be here as late as we need you to be. Don't complain about it. Don't expect a pat on the back. That's the job. If you're not willing to sacrifice your personal life for work, then there's the door."

It's not easy to prioritize your own life when you're in a service business and the hours can be pretty brutal. I instill in my staff that I believe family time is important, and we need to prioritize that the same way we prioritize client meetings. I don't want people to feel like they have to miss out on Little League games, dance recitals, or date nights because they can't get away from the office. We should be able to cover for one another.

We recently opened an office in New Jersey and won nearly $9 million in business for that location in the first few months. I told the leaders starting the office, "Hire the team that you need. Don't worry about being fiscally responsible right now. Get people in here that fit our culture and can do the work to make sure that you don't burn out."

They were stunned. They had come from a large agency where margin was king, and they were expected to grind themselves to the bone to grow the business while maintaining a certain profit margin. Encouraging them to not worry about profit because I didn't want them to overwork themselves freed them to focus on the work and finding the right people to grow the company. I don't want people to be ruled by profit margin because that stifles creativity. I know that talented people will produce when they are supported, and as a result, the money will come.

HOW WE SHOW EMPLOYEES WE CARE

There's typically a lot of turnover in the ad business. It's easy to move from one agency to another. Many agencies are located close together, and people can jump around for more pay, a better title, and other benefits. Obviously, every time you lose people, it causes disruption at the client level and at the team level. You have to recruit and train new people, get them up to speed, and build the relationship with the team and clients. It costs time and money.

The advertising business is not for the faint of heart. Our industry is known for tough hours, deadlines, stress, weekend work, night work, and travel. I do everything I can to take some of the burden off the people who work for me and make them feel embraced, supported, valued, and respected so they want to work with us for a long time.

As I've mentioned earlier, people are our most valuable asset; 80 percent of Fingerpaint's costs are people related, and our creative and strategic output is the only thing we are judged on. So once we have great people, it's important we nurture and grow them so that they stay with the company and continue to produce great work for our customers.

We've created an all-encompassing approach to benefits that recognizes that every employee has different needs and goals and strives to reach each and every one in a meaningful way. Not every benefit is significant for each employee, but the package combines to let every single person at Fingerpaint know that we care about them.

Here is a high-level overview of the benefits we provide:

1. **We pay 100 percent of the employee's and their family's health insurance.** We don't make employees pay a percentage of premiums or pay for their dependents. We cover them. This sends a clear message: when you're a part of our family, you and yours are covered.

    Financially this affects each employee differently, but it relieves stress for everyone. For a married employee with kids, it could save them more than $10,000 a year. We have people in our company who have children with special needs, and it feels really nice for me to be able to take some of that financial burden away from them. For a single person with no kids, it may save them $3,000 a year, so it's less influential. But everyone knows that they are covered and can live without the stress of paying high medical insurance costs or making the tough choice between paying for insurance and paying other bills.

2. **We have a student loan repayment program.** Working with a company called Gradifi allows us to pay down the principal of our employees' loans. When I graduated from Syracuse in 1989, I had just under $15,000 in loans. Today, kids come out of school with loans ten times that size. Each month, we pay $100 on the principal for every employee's student loans. This benefit doesn't do

anything for employees who don't have loans, but for our employees who recently got out of school, it's a huge deal.

We have some employees in their late twenties with literally six figures of student loan debt. They're paying $2,000 a month for their loans, which is the equivalent of a mortgage payment in our neighborhood. While $100 a month may not sound like much, for somebody with $30,000 in student loans, it can mean the difference between making payments for more than ten years or being debt free in less than eight years.

3. **We provide free gym memberships through Planet Fitness.** We value our employees' health and want to take the stress off choosing to pay for a gym membership—they don't have to make the decision between money coming out of their pocket or their health.

4. **We give every employee their birthday off.** This requires just one day of someone's time being lost to us, and it means the world to them. Life is worth celebrating, and by giving employees their birthdays off, we demonstrate that we want them to prioritize their lives.

5. **We have a matching 401(k) plan.** We match 100 percent of contributions up to 3 percent of an employee's income, and in 2020, we're raising that to match 100 percent on up to 4 percent.

6. **We have a family leave plan.** We provide eight weeks of paid leave for moms and dads. That includes parents giving birth to a child as well as parents giving birth via a surrogate or adopting.

7. **We bring joy to the team.** We try to think, at every turn, How can we bring a little bit of joy to the staff? We constantly do things that make them feel recognized and rewarded. We have tickets to the Boston Red Sox, New York Yankees, and Philadelphia 76ers for the staff to use. I have a ski condo in Okemo Mountain in Vermont; I let the staff use it whenever they want. People take a couple of days off to go up there or use it on the weekends and have an awesome time skiing with their family or friends. We pay for the cleaning and say, "Just replace the toilet paper, paper towels, and soap for the next guests." We do this to recognize how hard everyone works. By working together, we can all get the most out of life.

8. **We offer month-long sabbaticals after five years of service.** Burnout is inevitable in a high-paced creative business, so after five years of service, we give each employee a full month off in addition to their regular vacation time. They have to take it all at once. We disconnect email from their phone, and they're off the grid for a month. We cover for them, and we let the clients know who is covering for them. The effects of this on our employees are incredible.

I learned the value of the sabbatical from my first company. Four years after I started the company, my creative director was burned out. It's really hard starting any company, let alone an ad agency. He was burning the candle at both ends. He was stressed and unhealthy, and he came to me and said, "Ed, I gotta quit. I can't do this."

I told him, "You've been killing yourself for years. Take August off. Just get far away from here. We'll cover for you. Come back after Labor Day, and if you still want to leave, I'll help you find another job."

He came back after a month and was a new person. Refreshed. Healthy. He'd lost some weight. Reconnected with his family. To be honest, it didn't even affect the company negatively. To him, it was life changing.

This has a huge impact on the quality of work we can produce—if this was any other ad agency, that amazing creative director would have just quit because he was burned out, or he would have gone through the motions because he was unhappy or unhealthy. Especially in the creative business, sometimes you need time to get away and to lift your head out of the InDesign file. Far too often companies obsessed with productivity forget that they are employing *people* who need caring.

Because of the success of the sabbatical with my creative director at my first company, we instituted sabbaticals as a standard for all Fingerpaint employees at the five-year mark. It shows the employees how much we care about them and that we want them to have a life outside the office.

It also shows everyone that the world will turn without you. Advertising tends to attract a lot of type A personalities who feel they can never let go of the wheel. By giving these sabbaticals, we show everyone that we're going to be fine without you for a bit. Go enjoy yourself. We'll cover for you. You can cover for me the next time I need to rest.

People tell me the first week of the sabbatical feels like a typical vacation. Then, the second week, they really start to decompress. The third week is a fantasy. Then, by week four, they tend to start missing work. They get bored and are eager to come back. When they return, they're excited and refreshed.

Whenever someone comes back, we ask them to present to our company what they did on their sabbaticals. It's really cool, and we all love to see what people did. It also reminds everyone that we can cover for each other—we can hold down the fort and help each other have an amazing, life-changing experience.

To that person, it feels like they've been gone forever. But to the team, it feels like they were barely gone—it takes two weeks before we even realize somebody's out, because we're all immersed in our own work. Before we know it, they're back. The reality is that it's twenty days of work, which is not make or break for the team, but it is transformational for the individual.

People often plan their sabbaticals a year in advance. People with kids may take a cross-country trip in the summer. Others stay home and read books they've always wanted to read. We've had an employee get their pilot's license. Another went to New Zealand and Australia for a month. We've had folks go backpacking for two weeks throughout Europe and then stay home and rest for two weeks, because you always need a vacation to recover from your vacation.

I love that I can show people that I value their hard work over five years and that I can give them and their family the opportunity to just get away and enjoy life. If somebody has a life epiphany, and they come back and say, "I'm going to open up an Italian ice stand in Honolulu," God bless them. If somebody takes a sabbatical and resigns two weeks later, I don't feel taken advantage of. I'm glad I was able to give that to them and wish them well. The vast majority of people come back energized and happy to be back at work.

THE REWARDS OF GIVING FAR OUTWEIGH THE COSTS

There's an old saying that what you give comes back to you tenfold. I've found that to be true for my business. The benefits I provide employees are a leap of faith, because they're expensive, but the growth the employees bring to our company far exceeds the cost. We spend almost $3 million a year paying 100 percent of employee health-care premiums. The student loan repayment program costs us over $100,000 a year, and the gym memberships cost $30,000. Giving everyone their birthdays off may cost us $250,000 a year in lost billable time.

We're at $60 million in revenue, and I could easily pocket $4 million or $5 million in soft costs, but I would rather give back to the people who make it all possible. It brings me a lot of joy and satisfaction to be able to provide that for people.

The goodwill that our caring builds among our staff is amazing. When I announced we would cover everyone's entire health-care premiums, there were employees literally crying in our office because it meant so much to them.

One of our employees has a daughter with a heart condition that required multiple surgeries when her daughter was just a baby. So this employee was very aware of health-care costs. She was over the moon about having her premiums covered. It probably saves her $10,000 a year, but I could have given her a $10,000 raise, and it wouldn't have had nearly the same impact emotionally as paying her health-care premiums. She felt valued and taken care of.

If I ask her to come in for a weekend for a big project, she'll happily come in. She won't think I'm asking her to miss time at home because I want to put an addition on my house or meet an earnings goal. She'll see it as, "I'm appreciative of this company. Absolutely, I'll come in and contribute."

For as much as we provide for our employees, advertising is still a hard business that requires a lot from people. Our positive culture doesn't mean that people don't get stressed out or that we don't work weekends or late nights at times. We do. That's the nature of advertising. We work hard, and we expect a lot from our people.

The way we set ourselves apart is by looking out for one another and appreciating people for their hard work, rather than just expecting it. We give extra comp time if people have been burning the midnight oil, and we place a premium on covering for each other so we can all prioritize our own lives.

Doing all of this builds loyalty to me and to my company. It's a lot easier for people to say, "Ed gave me his condo for a week, and I got to ski with my family. If I have to come in on Sunday to get this project out the door, he's not taking advantage of me. I want to be able to do this for the company." Of course, no one will ever be thrilled to come in to work on a weekend, but because our employees know we care for them, most of the time they're happy to contribute to the team instead of being disgruntled by the extra work.

As much as the benefits may cost us, there are a lot of hidden costs to not caring for employees; when you have to replace people every year or two, you have to recruit, train, and accept a learning curve as they get up to speed. But if you take care of your people, they grow with you and build relationships that lead to better work for us and our clients.

That's not to say we don't have turnover. Some people take the free health care and other benefits for granted, especially if they're new to the business.

> The way we set ourselves apart is by looking out for one another and appreciating people for their hard work, rather than just expecting it.

I have heard many times that we're a great second agency for people, because if someone's first job is here, they may not realize how special it is. But we have an excellent reputation on Glassdoor and very strong talent retention, especially at the senior levels. If somebody goes to another company, I can rest easy because at least

I know that we've done everything we can to make them feel like this is a special place.

I feel very proud of how we support the people in the company. Because the staff knows that we care about them as people, and not just as moneymakers, they actually work harder and produce more for us. On top of that, caring from the leadership team has also created a culture of employees caring for each other. For example, I was worried that the student loan payment program wouldn't be well received at the company because it doesn't affect everybody. But the reaction was unanimously positive. The sentiment among those not affected was, "That's awesome! It's so great that we can do that for people."

There's a sense of camaraderie that we're all in this together. Our young, single employees are glad we can pay the more expensive health-care premiums for those with families, and the older folks without student loans are happy we can help the younger employees. All of us pull for each other, which leads to better work and happier employees.

Jenny McKenna, one of our operations heads, says it better than I ever could: "The job is important because it's meaningful and fun, and the people we work with become our best friends, our family. So, I approach that team like I would my family—if someone has to be home because their wife's dad died, or because they have a new baby, or because their kid is going through something awful at school, we help out—I manage that team to help out, to cover, to fill in—so that we can all live our lives and do our work."

JOB SECURITY: NEVER LAYING PEOPLE OFF

The staff knows that I've never laid anybody off in more than twenty years of running companies. I'm very proud of that, and I hope I can always make that claim. I never want anybody to lose their job if they are good at what they do. I am very passionate about that. I see my job as making sure that we have a constant pipeline of work and that we're well diversified, so that losing a client doesn't put us in jeopardy. Our largest client represents 13 percent of our business, which provides a lot of security.

I value our people and their families so much that if we have a bad month or we lose a client, they know that their jobs aren't in jeopardy and that I'm going to figure out a way to keep them employed, even if we operate at a loss for a while, so they can feel safe. They know that I'm not going to sell them out. It's not just about making money for me.

I've gotten offers as high as $170 million to sell Fingerpaint, but I don't need an exit strategy. I love this company. I want to stay so that I can keep guard over the culture we've created and use the money we make to give back to our people and our communities.

PHILANTHROPY

Caring for others outside the business is vital to producing a positive culture. This is an extension of the empathy we show each other at work and adds meaning to everything we do. I want our employees to see how fortunate we are to have jobs with good incomes and to work with people we like. I strive to create an environment where people don't take it for granted and that we're constantly in a position to give back to those less fortunate in our communities.

We have a full-time philanthropist on staff, which is unusual for an agency our size. We try to be do-gooders, not out of a sense of obligation or to be on the cover of the newspaper, but because we feel it's all part of caring for people and showing an appreciation for everyone—not just those who could help our business.

We give our dollars, and we give our time. We have staff members who volunteer on charity boards and lend marketing expertise. We replaced our summer company picnic with a company-wide philanthropy day. In 2018, our philanthropy day was a project called Operation Lunch Lady, which focused on helping kids who rely on school for food. During the summer, those children can no longer go to school for breakfast and lunch, so we partnered with an organization that sends food to them. We created sixty-five thousand meals to send to kids. In 2019, we did it again, this time packing eighty thousand meals.

My wife and I pledged a million dollars of our own money to help build a homeless shelter in our hometown. We recently bought a new bloodmobile for the upstate New York Red Cross. I've sat on numerous boards for charity organizations. The staff sees me putting my money where my mouth is, but they also see the company getting behind it, and it makes them feel great. They come to us with organizations that are important to them, to see if we'll support them. Ninety-nine percent of the time, we will. It can be anything from somebody running a 5K to raise money to getting involved in a local charity that is particularly meaningful to them. When one of our creative team member's thirteen-year-old dog passed away, Fingerpaint made a donation to a rescue group in their honor.

We don't give back for a business purpose; we do it because it makes us feel proud to do good in the world. But as with every other instance of giving that comes back positively, our philanthropy does benefit our business. Our philanthropy helps us attract employees, because people want to make a difference.

On top of being a great recruitment tool, our commitment to philanthropy and caring limits the risk of unethical behavior at every level of the company. If our employees know we value doing right over making money, they know that we'd never ask them to do anything that would be unethical, and that if they see a problem, they'll work to fix it to ensure that we do right by each other and by our customers.

PERSONAL CARING MEANS MORE THAN WHITE-GLOVE SERVICE

The best indicator of how a company will care about you is how the employees care for each other. Years ago, Bank of America held an RFP for a $120 million per year contract. It narrowed its search to two large agencies and spent a day at each agency. One of the requirements it gave the agencies was to host a team dinner for Bank of America's team to interact with the agency teams.

One of the agencies, a massive company with a reputation for being upper crust, laid out the red carpet for Bank of America's team. It had white-glove service, fancy linen tablecloths, candelabras, crystal, and china. All employees who attended were dressed to the nines for this very expensive and formal dinner that was meant to impress.

The other agency took a completely different approach, built around caring and customer service. It had their members wear bright and colorful Bank of America shirts and had them spread out throughout the event specifically to guide the Bank of America people through the building. If somebody needed to know where the restroom was or which elevator to take, there was a friendly agency employee right there. It didn't cost any money to do that, but it showed a level of humanity and down-to-earth customer service that resonated.

That agency's dinner was customized to show it understood the customer. It set up stations with food from every state in which Bank of America had a branch. For Louisiana, there was a crawfish station. For New York, there were steaks. Florida, Cuban sandwiches. It went out of its way to be inclusive of all walks of life.

> **Because of our culture of caring, our employees treat our clients with the same level of caring that we show each other.**

The CEO of Bank of America, who was eating at one of the tables, commented, "Do you realize we have a branch in every one of these areas?" The employees started laughing. "Yeah, that was the point." Bank of America's team was so impressed by how well thought out and caring the entire day was that they awarded the agency the contract.

EMPATHY TO OUR STAFF LEADS TO EMPATHY TO OUR CUSTOMERS

Because of our culture of caring, our employees treat our clients with the same level of caring that we show each other. As a result, we lose very little business. Typically, when agencies get fired, it's because clients feel that the agency is taking them for granted, not providing new ideas, and treating the client like a cash cow and not a priority.

Our positive culture leads to us caring about our clients as people and going that extra mile to care for them, working weekends when we have to and treating them well. We've had people push their sabbaticals off for a few months because they didn't feel like it was a good time for them to leave their teammates or customers. We don't ask them to do that, but our people care about one another and are proud of the work we create and the clients we support.

If one of our clients has a major life event, we celebrate it. If someone needs support because they're having a rough patch, we support them. We become an extension of their own inner circle. They know that we care. As a result, we forge lasting relationships that deliver positive growth for ourselves and our customers.

Of course, for this to work most effectively, we have to connect with our clients early on, and that involves both parties setting the right tone for the relationship from the start.

CHAPTER FIVE

ESTABLISHING A POSITIVE RELATIONSHIP

Congratulations! You've selected an agency! The opening stages of the relationship present the best opportunity you'll ever have to build a healthy working partnership. You're excited because you have a new partner. The agency is excited because it just won the pitch. Everybody is fired up and ready to go.

You have to harness that enthusiasm to lay the groundwork for a positive relationship, so that everybody carries that same level of zeal throughout the everyday grind in the years to come. Everything in the relationship rests on the foundation of how you introduce it. If you set up a partnership based on mutual caring, it will absolutely make a difference for you in crunch time.

Years ago, we were helping a client launch an oncology drug. That client was very demanding but also took the time to really invest in us right from the start. They were understanding and attentive and weren't afraid to spend money to do the work the right way. They understood the value of creative work, so we never wanted to let them down, no matter how challenging the project.

One year, we were preparing their product to go to market and had to submit all the informational materials to the FDA in thirteen separate languages. There was a hard-and-fast deadline they had to meet from the FDA before the product could go to market, because if the drug is used incorrectly, it can be deadly. When we learned that the deadline was the day after Thanksgiving, it was crunch time.

We knew this wasn't a client that would impose a deadline without a good reason—they needed us to go above and beyond, and we went into high gear. During the weeks leading up to Thanksgiving, we worked really hard to get everything done, but on Thanksgiving Day, we had an enormous amount of paperwork that had to be collated and organized. I had to call in nearly the entire agency on Thanksgiving morning to collate the submissions for the FDA so that somebody could drive a van full of the materials to drop off at the FDA in Maryland before the deadline Friday afternoon.

I felt like a terrible leader because I had worked these people to the bone leading up to Thanksgiving, and I couldn't even give them Thanksgiving morning off. But everybody came in. I was amazed that no one complained, and no one called in sick. From top to bottom, we all put the time in, and it galvanized us as an agency because we had people at all levels of the company, from senior executives to entry-level employees, collating pages side by side. We were laughing and joking, and we got it all done in a few hours, so everybody was home by eleven o'clock in the morning.

The client was not aware at the time that we came in on Thanksgiving to finish everything for them. When they found out, they were blown away. They made a video thanking us and sent it to everybody on the team and also sent a bunch of care packages to the office. They took the core team to a spa for a few days to thank them for all their hard work. The marketing executives paid for the spa themselves, rather than running it through the company, because they were so touched on a personal level by what we had done.

It was a wonderful learning experience for me because I really saw how much a caring client can charge up and motivate an agency. The level of caring established early on in the relationship built a trust within our team that this deadline was important and a feeling on our side that we didn't want to let the client down.

To this day we still work with the executives from that assignment, who have since gone on to other companies. We stayed friends with them, and they know they can rely on us when they need to. For a relationship to be that strong, the partnership needs to get off on the right foot.

CREATING ONGOING SUCCESS

SETTING EXPECTATIONS FOR ONGOING SUCCESS

We built this graphic to show what clients can expect from us as a partner and what an agency should expect from a customer to have a fruitful partnership. I'll quickly go through what each bullet point means so that you can use this as a guide to establish a profitable agency-customer partnership.

EXPECTATIONS FOR YOUR AGENCY

Be strategic: An agency's job is to lead the brand direction and figure out the right message, positioning, and the best ways to roll the product out. We shouldn't just be a tactical shop, producing sales aids, websites, and virtual reality trade show booths without a strategic overlay of why we're making them. Every piece of work should function together to achieve a specific aim.

Whenever a client suggests a tactic, such as sending a certain number of emails in a campaign or creating a trade show booth, the first question your agency should ask is: Why? What is the reasoning behind it? Let's look at the results of past work and analyze other relevant data to make strategic decisions about what approach to take. We take a much higher-level approach to the brand as opposed to just going through the motions.

Be present: You're busy, and so is the agency. It's easy nowadays to be only partially present at any moment, because while we are on a conference call with you, we might receive thirty emails. So we promise that while we're meeting, we're present. We're not checking our phones or reading emails while you are talking, as that would result in us missing important feedback.

Deliver what's right: We will not produce anything that may get you, as the customer, in trouble from a medical, regulatory, or legal standpoint. We will make sure that we live your brand and are true to the brand values.

Challenge ideas: It's important for an agency to engage in healthy debate with you to find the best solutions, rather than simply being yay-sayers. When we disagree with something, we'll respectfully push back on an idea to arrive at the best course of action.

Be transparent: In everything we do, we will be transparent. We have an open-book policy so that you know what projects we're working on, who is working on what, how long it will take, how much it costs, and why we're doing it that way. Transparency from an agency helps eliminate surprises and keeps everybody on the same page.

You should expect cost transparency from an agency. Advertising can be expensive. We've done websites for $10,000, and we've done websites for more than $1 million, depending on the complexity. There are many different ways to charge for work. Your agency needs to help you understand how those rates are calculated so that you understand why decisions are made, such as when to involve senior-level talent and when to delegate to junior people, to ensure the right balance of quality and cost.

The most irritating thing an agency can do is come in with a surprise cost that pushes the project over budget, so it's very important that we provide regular updates to you on each project and its budget. For example, if we're 50 percent through a project but 80 percent through the budget, that's a problem. By being transparent, we can get ahead of it and explore: Why is the project not tracking with the budget? Where are things going off the rails? How do we get it back on track? If you have requested changes that weren't originally in the plan, it's important for the agency to highlight the fact that these changes affect the budget, instead of that being a surprise when the bill comes. There has to be an open and honest view of the cost and what's going into the work for everyone to be happy with the outcome.

Be proactive: Agencies do a disservice to the brand if they act only as order takers and do not push the envelope, come up with creative ideas that the client may not have asked for, and provide solutions above and beyond the scope of the assignment. It's important for an agency to be forward thinking and not just wait for you to call us with requests. We should constantly look for ways to help your brand. You should expect your agency to be proactive, and they should know you expect that.

Be respectful of your time and resources: You are busy, and you don't have time to sit in meetings for days and days. You should have to tell an agency something only once and not have to repeat yourself. Everything we do should add value and not be a drain, giving you the most possible return on your investment of time and resources.

To streamline communication for you as a client, the account manager is your main point of contact at the agency and acts as a quarterback for all the people involved. Together with the project manager, who tracks budgets and timelines, they hold the agency teams accountable so that you don't have to spend too much time managing the agency.

So if you have a question on budget or timing, or if you're not happy with the creative, you can express that to your advocate at the agency without fear of hurting people's feelings. You can tell the account manager, "This doesn't look right," or "This isn't on strategy." Then it's up to the account team to rally the troops at the agency to fix it.

With that said, you will benefit from working with the extended team at times, so the creative folks can hear directly from you what they're trying to accomplish. Including the creative people in certain meetings will actually streamline work if handled in a way that is respectful of your time and resources.

REQUIREMENTS FOR YOUR AGENCY

Give constructive feedback: We always want you to be honest with us and provide detail. Don't just tell us you don't like something; explain why you don't like it and some aspects you do like, so that we can get to the heart of what we need to do to improve the work. We have thick skins, and we welcome honest constructive criticism. With direction from you about what does and doesn't work, we can take the project forward effectively.

Commit to quality: The best clients respect our process and are mindful that our recommendations are in service of making the work better, not in service of making the agency the most money.

My prior agency worked with Magic Johnson on his HIV foundation and with GlaxoSmithKline, which had several products to treat HIV. When choosing a photographer, we recommended the client hire Herb Ritts, a very famous fashion photographer who has since passed away. Herb charged $125,000 for the day for the photo shoot. It was an expensive recommendation for the client, but we didn't make any money by suggesting Herb—we just knew he would make the work better.

The photos Herb took were in black and white and were absolutely distinctive. Magic was thrilled with the work, and it educated a ton of patients and won a ton of creative awards. It was one of the most effective and powerful ads that GlaxoSmithKline has ever done. A lot of that was because of Herb's vision. Another client may have been willing to only do a cheaper photo shoot with a lesser-known photographer, and the work would not have moved the market the

Earvin Johnson, diagnosed with HIV in 1991.

For me, staying healthy with HIV is about a few basic things:

A positive attitude. Partnering with my doctor. Taking medicine every day.

One of the keys to living with HIV is finding a treatment plan that may be right for you – then sticking with it. For some people, getting through the first few months of HIV therapy can be tough, so discuss it with your doctor. The decisions you make today can make a huge difference for years to come.

For information about living with HIV, call 1-888-TREAT HIV, or visit www.TreatHIV.com.

GlaxoSmithKline

©2002 The GlaxoSmithKline Group of Companies All rights reserved. Printed in USA HIV226R0 October 2002

same way. The client committed to quality, and it paid off. Patients within the HIV community were positively influenced in meaningful ways.

Be open minded: Our job is to provide ideas that you haven't considered. But even the best ideas are worthless unless you are open to try things you haven't done before. That's not to say we expect you to accept every suggestion—healthy debate is crucial to success. We ask you to be open minded, because our recommendations will be grounded in our expertise and what we believe is right for the brand.

> Even the best ideas are worthless unless you are open to try things you haven't done before.

Provide clarity and exposure: Provide your agency access to the information we need to do our jobs. Make sure that you include the agency as a real member of the team. Introduce us to members of your extended team and to your sales groups so we can understand what the sales teams are up against. Allow us to sit in on research and be a fly on the wall for plan-of-action meetings and national sales meetings to give us the insight that we need to do our job.

There can be a natural hesitancy on your part to include your agency, because you may feel that every time you call the agency, you're on the clock, especially if you've been burned by an agency before. However, restricting communication to save money falls into the category of being penny wise and pound foolish. Having more communication usually lowers the overall cost of a project, because collaborating with the agency can make the work better and decrease the time that it takes to develop the work.

Agencies need to be strategically immersed in the brand, and the more that you can share to help the agency understand the commercial challenges that lie ahead, the more we can help you meet those goals. Information that can help might include the following:

- Market research

- Clinical trials or scientific studies that may not be published yet

- Scientific data

- Consumer insights and research that you've done in the past

- Sales goals

- Price sensitivity data

- Consumer preference data

Allowing your agency into the inner sanctum and providing it access to any tools that you have that it couldn't get on its own will help the agency to be a true commercial partner and not just a vendor producing a series of tactics.

Be available and diligent: We understand that you are busy, but you need to carve out the time to invest in your agency's success for us to come through for you. When clients do not make time for an agency's questions, it can cause frustration on both sides because the agency may be waiting for answers from a client, and the client may be waiting for work from the agency. It's a catch-22 where each side is waiting for the other, but no one is talking. By being available for consistent communication early on, you can streamline the work and avoid many of these problems.

There's a fundamental availability an agency needs from you as the client to deliver quality work. If your agency sends something to review and a timeline for a few days to review it, you can't send it back two weeks later and expect us to stay on time. When we meet, we need you to be present, just as our team will be. Of course, as covered above, the agency must respect your time so that when you are available, we use your time effectively.

It's very important to make time for regular communication at the start of the relationship and beyond. Have weekly status calls and monthly face-to-face meetings to start, so you can connect on what we're working on, the status of projects, and how we're tracking to the budget. The key is to assess if everything is going according to plan or if there are issues you need to address, such as budget concerns, or team members not jelling.

EXPECTATIONS FOR BOTH PARTIES

Work together: Both parties need to commit to working together as a unified team. A few years ago, we were working on a copromoted product, which means that there were two pharmaceutical companies responsible for marketing the product, which was a drug for erectile dysfunction.

The two brand teams did not get along well, and we couldn't get them to agree on the strategy. As a result, our agency was spinning our wheels, producing work that met one client's strategy but not the other's. We'd redo it to meet the other's strategy and lose the first client's buy-in. The nearly endless ping-ponging revisions that resulted meant that work that should have cost $50,000 ended up being $300,000.

I felt it was malpractice not to say anything. We had exhausted every option at that point, and our team was frustrated because they were revising things over and over, and the work was not getting done. I felt the client should not have been spending that much money on work, and my teams should have been able to produce work that we were proud of.

So I met with the two clients' leaders and said, "I wanted to make you two aware of this. I'm not trying to throw anybody under a bus, but right now, the relationship isn't working, and it's costing you both hundreds of thousands of dollars in agency fees because your teams aren't on the same page."

One of the executives thanked me and said, "You didn't have to do that, and I appreciate you bringing it to our attention. We'll work together to get our teams playing nicer in the sandbox."

The other client was upset because he thought I was blaming his team. It was interesting to see the two perspectives. One was a more seasoned leader who understood the importance of transparency and honest discussion, and the other was more worried about how it would make him look. It's easy from that story to see which client is going to have more success empowering their agency to produce better work at a lower cost.

Be honest with one another: Being true partners means sharing the good, bad, and ugly and evaluating what works and what doesn't. It's important that the senior leadership of the agency has a very close relationship with the senior leadership of the client. The senior leaders need to spend time together and look out for one another to build trust and understanding that everybody's coming from the right place, and at the end of the day, we all want the same thing—helping patients while also growing our businesses.

That senior-level connection becomes crucial when there are problems; if either side is frustrated with something, the leaders on both sides can work behind the scenes to get things right on their side and to properly motivate both teams.

Define success: For an agency to hit a goal and for you to effectively evaluate them, you have to define success for the project. Success can be quantitative or qualitative and will vary for each client, but it has to be clear.

For a product that hasn't launched yet, success may be to develop the most strategic breakthrough creative material. Or, if a product is launching, the goal can be to achieve a certain number of patients trialed on the product over a certain period of time. Or we may want to ensure that the physicians with the highest patient populations for the product all try it in the first sixty days. Of course, all these goals will be within the confines of what's in the best interest of the patients. Doing right by patients is absolutely critical, and Fingerpaint and our clients always honor that. It's an ethical necessity.

Set expectations: To get the best work from your agency, you have to set expectations for the way that you want to reach success. Every company has different preferences for how they'd like to advertise. Some are very conservative creatively and do not want to stir the pot. Others want to push the envelope and be disruptive.

Once you've selected an agency, review the pitch with the team members and give feedback. Tell them what you liked, what missed the mark, and why. Let the agency know if you've tried a strategy already that was suggested during the pitch and how effective it was or was not. Anything you can do to be up front and honest with each other is extremely helpful.

Every time we start a relationship with a new client, we invite its marketing executives to spend a few days with us walking through how we work so that they can immerse themselves in what everyone does. We show them what the copywriters do, what editors handle, what medical writers focus on, what the web team is responsible for, and so on.

This walk-through is very helpful in setting expectations. When you hire a new agency, ask the team members to walk you through how they work. Especially if you do not have a lot of experience working with ad agencies, you can learn quite a bit that will help you as work is being produced.

This will help you understand why some things that seem simple may actually take longer than expected. For example, many times we get phone calls asking us to change a paragraph or two on the website, which may seem like it can be done in ten minutes. However, it might actually take a few hours because it has to be drafted and then edited. Then the medical team has to ensure accuracy. Next it has to be posted on the website. Finally, it has to be tested to make sure it didn't mess up any of the web page programming. There may be design elements around the paragraph that have to be tweaked to make the page still look good. Unless you've worked as a creator, it's hard to know all that's involved, so your expectations may be different than reality.

Typically, problems occur between two groups when one doesn't appreciate what the other is going through. There's nothing worse from our perspective than having a client that is clueless about the amount of effort it takes to get work done and makes an artificial deadline—"I need this by Monday at 8:00 a.m." We work all weekend only to find out the client is on vacation the next week, and the work is just going to sit on their desk for a week.

Both sides have to work in the beginning of the relationship to better understand where each side is coming from, what they need to do their jobs effectively, and what their pain points have been in the past so that we can work to avoid them in the future. Here are some questions we ask new clients:

- What did you like and dislike about working with agencies?

- When you've had great relationships with agencies, what's been the key?

- What do you value?

- Do you want to be involved in the development of the creative and the strategy?

- How often do you want to have meetings?

I encourage you to provide your agency with the answers to those questions up front and ask your agency a similar set of questions to understand what makes a good client and what makes a bad one. If you can understand from an agency's perspective what helps it work better, you will know how to keep the agency's team motivated and to empower them to do the best work they're capable of.

We want to make you successful, and it's human nature that people will work harder for those they respect and like.

Be collaborative. Be willing to consider your agency a true partner and not just a vendor. A good agency will bring as much to the brand as your internal team will. It's important to understand the effort all the people at the agency will put into your brand and to set a tone of collaboration. We've had clients present to our entire agency about the challenges that we would face together, and that goes such a long way in getting the team on board.

If your team can put a face on the patients that we're trying to help, it's a game changer. If we're working on a product for children with cancer or another serious illness, tell us some stories about parents you've met and what they're going through. Taking the time to embrace the agency and say, "You're on the team now; this is our mission, and we need you," will show the agency that you value its team and will make them want to work harder for you.

SET A TONE OF CARING, AND YOUR AGENCY WILL DELIVER FOR YOU

The key to achieving all the previous points and setting the right relationship is to spend a significant amount of time up front getting to know each other as people. Hold team-building events and lunches or dinners at the start of the relationship to connect on a human level so that everyone has an understanding of what's going on in each other's worlds. There's a connection that comes from getting to know one another as people so that we can have empathy for each other as we begin to build the working relationship.

A key reason we don't lose many clients may sound cliché, but it's because we form close bonds as people. At the end of the day, our job is not only to move market share, but it's also to help you advance in your career. We want to make you successful, and it's human nature that people will work harder for those they respect and like.

That human connection also helps both sides when things go wrong. Everybody makes mistakes. If we miss something, or if you forget to send us some information, we give each other the benefit of the doubt because we know each other as people. We're not perfect, but we continually strive to be better, and we know that the other side will always do what's right.

When you invest the time to understand and value your agency team, they will go above and beyond to make things happen for you. I saw from my team firsthand that a foundation of trust and caring between agency and client means we'll even happily come in on Thanksgiving morning for you.

Of course, getting the relationship off on the right foot is just the beginning. In the next chapter, I'll outline how you can continue to foster the positive relationship throughout the partnership.

CHAPTER SIX

HOW TO EMBRACE AND NURTURE A POSITIVE CULTURE

A lot of people hear the words "positive culture" and picture companies pandering to millennials with fun perks like ping-pong tables or beer at the office. As we've discussed, a positive culture is about more than benefits—it's about caring relationships between people, and it has to start with you as a leader showing your people, including vendors, partners, and the community, that you care about them.

Recently I had a quick business trip on the East Coast, and due to scheduling conflicts, I needed to charter a plane for eight o'clock in the morning. It's pretty expensive to charter a plane even if you're going only a few hundred miles, so usually the plane is there waiting for you right on time. I arrived at the airport, and the plane was not there. I waited about ten minutes, but nobody showed up.

I called the charter company and said, "I scheduled a flight at eight, and it's ten after eight, but there's nobody here." The woman said, "Oh my God, let me check." She came back and was panicked because she didn't properly file the scheduling slip, and the plane wasn't coming. She started to cry. "Oh my God. I just had somebody in my family pass away, and I'm so spastic. I'm so sorry; I'll send somebody right now. It'll be there at ten o'clock, and I'll waive part of your bill. I'm so, so sorry."

I called my assistant and rearranged some of my appointments. It was just two hours and didn't cause any major problems, but I knew how bad the woman from the charter company felt. I said to my assistant, "Do me a favor and send flowers to this woman with a note that says, 'Thank you for fixing the issue. Everybody makes mistakes. Please don't sweat it.'"

At the end of the day, I received a call from the woman at the charter company. She said, "I can't believe you did that. I should be sending you flowers." I told her, "You owned it. You didn't make up an excuse. You fixed the problem, and everybody makes mistakes. It was only two hours. I appreciate you. It's OK." She wrote me a long thank-you card, and it's clear that the small gesture I made sending her flowers had a huge impact on her.

I try to look at all the ways that I can make people's lives a little bit better, whether they're my employees or others I come in contact with. When you treat people around you with care, positivity comes back to you when you need it.

DON'T SET IT AND FORGET IT—WHAT TO FOCUS ON TO ENHANCE POSITIVE CULTURE

A positive culture isn't something you can just set at the start of a relationship and forget. You have to continually look for ways to show the people around you that you care.

If you want to benefit from the positivity you generate at the beginning of the relationship with your agency, you need to do the following:

- Be transparent

- Practice the art of giving feedback

- Communicate good and bad news openly

- Include your agency as a real partner

- Recognize and reward hard work

- Admit shortcomings and strive to improve

- Present a greater purpose with philanthropy

- Create an atmosphere of "we're all in this together"

BE TRANSPARENT

Transparency within your team is important—and with your agency too. Tell us where we need to improve as an agency and where you think we're doing a great job.

It's important for your leadership team and the agency's leaders to keep an open and honest dialogue. Have regular dinners and calls to talk about the status of the business and areas of opportunity. When the relationship between a client and agency goes bad, it often is because one side or both don't have a forum to express concerns, and frustration builds without an outlet to turn things around. That connection with the leadership teams on both sides, both committed to transparency, is vital to keeping the relationship strong and giving each side the opportunity to iron out issues constructively.

Giving your team and agency partners the ability to ask questions is vital as well. We don't have individual offices at Fingerpaint, so there isn't a hierarchical fear stopping people from walking over to my cube and asking me a question about anything. Even if you have offices in your company, making yourself available to your staff and partners and being truly transparent will help you maintain a positive connection with your people.

PRACTICE THE ART OF GIVING FEEDBACK

There is an art to giving effective feedback to your agency. Creatives can be temperamental when it comes to criticism of their work, because they work very hard on it, and there is a subjective flair to creative work.

When clients simply say, "I don't like this one. This one might work, but we need to do some things to it," and they do not elaborate, it can cause tension with the creative team. The feedback feels subjective rather than constructive.

A more effective way to give feedback is to start by sharing what you had a positive reaction to and why and what you had a negative reaction to and why. Providing the reasoning behind a detail that you like or dislike will help the creative team not only address that specific issue but apply that logic to other aspects of the work going forward.

Another very effective tool when you feel the creative team missed the mark is to ask the team, "What were you going for here?" If you then listen to the creative team, you'll get a sense of if they misunderstood the message behind the advertisement or if it is simply a creative execution issue—an important distinction that can help you and the creative team set a course to hit the mark on the next version.

COMMUNICATE GOOD AND BAD NEWS OPENLY

The companies with the best cultures share good news and bad news with the team, helping them understand the levers of the business. We share why we make decisions, we celebrate wins, we explain what went wrong when there are issues, and we answer questions.

At Fingerpaint, we have staff meetings at each office every month. We've had people join us from other agencies who told us the only time they did company-wide staff meetings was when they lost a big client or there were going to be layoffs. Naturally, people got nervous whenever they saw a staff meeting pop up on their calendars.

We host meetings regularly as part of our commitment to transparency, to share good news, and to answer questions in an open, honest forum. We celebrate our victories as a team during these meetings, and each office revels in the others' successes.

> Regularly celebrating wins and analyzing losses with the whole team goes a long way toward fostering togetherness and collective growth.

We demonstrate how we won, and our people get a chance to show appreciation for each other. Conversely, if we lose business, we get everybody together and say, "We didn't get this one. Here's where we fell short. It's over. Let's move on," and learn from our failures without dwelling on them. Regularly celebrating wins and analyzing losses with the whole team goes a long way toward fostering togetherness and collective growth.

INCLUDE YOUR AGENCY AS A REAL PARTNER

The most successful marketing leaders treat their agencies as part of their staff. They include them in research, sales, and plan-of-action meetings, not just at the start of the relationship but continuously, so that the agency team can stay current with the company's goals. The more the agency is included, the better we can do our jobs.

Spending time at the agency and sharing the goals of the brand with the extended team is very healthy. By continually expressing your mission and success with your agency's team, you show that you value them, and they'll walk through fire for you in return.

You have to be invested in the agency, make the time to cultivate relationships, and be present to have a successful partnership. A lot of clients say they're too busy for the agency and can't invest the time to work closely together. That is a huge missed opportunity, because if the relationship with your agency works properly, it can do more to increase sales of your brand than nearly any other initiative.

One major competitive advantage you can harness in the health-care space is connecting your agency team with your legal, regulatory, and medical teams, who have the tough job of ensuring that everything communicated is legally and medically accurate.

If the agency's creative team and your medical, regulatory, and legal teams don't work closely together, the relationship often turns adversarial: those teams see the creative team as trying to slip something by them, while the creative team sees the others as campaign killers.

At Fingerpaint, we make a point to include your medical, regulatory, and legal teams early in the creative process; we share rough concepts with them and ask, "We're thinking about going in this direction—what do you guys think?" They value that we bring them into the process early, and it makes them feel that we're in it together and not opposing forces, which means they'll look for solutions with us to the creative challenges and not ways to shoot things down.

RECOGNIZE AND REWARD HARD WORK

Treating your agency with respect and making a point to recognize the team members' long hours and hard work will go a long way toward building goodwill with your team. We've had clients send us dinner when they know we're working late nights for them. Little things like that can supercharge the relationship.

Internally, I do this for my team whenever I know they're going above and beyond. In January this year, we were absolutely slammed, so I bought lunch every day for everyone in the office. Pizza one day, salads the next, Chipotle the third, then Subway, and so on. I did this as a tip of the cap to the staff to say, "I know how busy you are. I don't expect you to never leave the office, but if you have to work through lunch, the least I can do is buy you a sandwich."

One of our senior teams had four major pitches in a short period of time, so they were working overtime for quite a while. Once the pitches were over, we gave each of them and their significant others a weekend at a nice hotel in Manhattan, along with dinner and a show.

If you can show appreciation to your people when they do go above and beyond, they'll feel that you care about them, and they'll give it all they have for you when you need them.

It doesn't take a financial investment to make people feel appreciated. You can find ways to acknowledge them that are creative. We have a "Gao Award" at Fingerpaint, which is a peer-to-peer award named after the world's first finger painter, Gao Qipei of the eighteenth century. Once a month at a staff meeting, someone wins the Gao Award for embodying our values and going above and beyond. The award itself is a little statue, and the person who wins it has to present it to someone new the next month. Companies with healthy cultures develop internal traditions to celebrate their people and rally everybody around their values.

ADMIT SHORTCOMINGS AND STRIVE TO IMPROVE

None of us is perfect, but it's important we acknowledge where we need to improve. The worst thing you can do for employee morale is to try to sell your people on a negative part of the working experience at your company. You have to listen to feedback from your team and work to fix problems instead of simply saying, "This is how we are. If you don't like it, you can go somewhere else."

We revamped our maternity and paternity policy because, when I visited one of our offices, we had four pregnant employees, and they politely told me our maternity plan was not good enough. I examined it, agreed with them, and in two days, we changed our maternity policy.

Employees have to see that their concerns are being addressed. They may not always like the resolution, but you have to listen to them and have an honest and transparent communication about issues if you want to foster a culture that people believe in.

One of the things we struggle with at Fingerpaint is career progression, in large part because we don't have a title-based hierarchy. Rather than run from the problem, we're working to address it. We've put a major focus with our human resources and leadership teams to roll out a career progression plan by functional area, so that people understand their opportunities and how they can advance their careers.

We've hired a training manager who will customize training per person based on their developmental needs and provide group trainings. We sponsor employees to seek outside training, as there are so many amazing resources out there. Some of our IT staff like going to the Apple conference every year in California, so we send them there to be around like-minded people and learn

Employees have to see that their concerns are being addressed.

about the latest Apple technology. We continually look for ways to provide opportunities for our employees to grow.

Most agencies have very layered, incredibly bureaucratic systems that have clear career progression maps, but we don't want to go that route, because a title and a small bump in pay isn't real progression. In a lot of ways, having no titles frees us. We can move someone up a career progression very quickly when they demonstrate they can perform.

A former employee built our accounting and finance function from the ground up. She joined us at an entry-level salary in an administrative capacity, and within the span of five years, she excelled so much that she was doing the work of a traditional CFO—so we tripled her salary. That doesn't happen in a bureaucratic system. We are working to maintain the freedom that the title-free system provides while improving career progression paths for our employees.

Still, we recognize the flaws in our career progression plan and work to improve our training to help our people reach more responsibility and reap more financial benefits. That type of self-reflection and corrective action is crucial to sustaining a positive culture.

PRESENT A LARGER PURPOSE WITH PHILANTHROPY

A continuous commitment to philanthropy is absolutely vital. There's a popular sentiment in the marketplace that millennials want to work for a company that gives back. My experience is that so do fifty-year-olds. People of all ages want to be part of an organization that they believe in, which is why we put a lot of effort into community outreach programs. It makes everybody feel blessed and that we are making a meaningful impact on the world.

Doing good in your community also allows you to express who you are without the confines of a financial goal, which can be very beneficial in showing your employees, partners, and customers what you stand for.

Our work with the Concussion Legacy Foundation to help prevent CTE in kids and adults provides an opportunity for the staff to embrace a cause simply because we believe in the science. It allows us to show our people we care about the world we live in. The commercial we created for the foundation also shows our customers that we are creative, we stand up for what we believe in, and we are good at what we do.

I went to a McDonald's drive-through recently, and I had the Fingerpaint logo on the side of my pickup truck. The woman who gave me my food saw the Fingerpaint logo and said, "I hear that's a great company. They do wonderful things for the community." She had no idea I owned the company, and her kind words made my month. That's really what my mission is—to create a company that can have a positive impact on the community.

By presenting a larger purpose to your people, you can instill a sense of pride in the company and a feeling that what you do matters, which will lead to incredible success for your business.

CREATE AN ATMOSPHERE OF "WE'RE ALL IN THIS TOGETHER"

It's important to be connected to your team as a leader and to do the things that you ask your team to do. If we have a philanthropy day, our team sees the company leaders right there with them, side by side and helping, which is very important because a fundamental factor of our culture is that everybody counts. Everybody has a voice. That's why we don't have titles or offices. We don't have an us and them mentality, the worker bees and the ivory tower office executives—we're all in this together.

> A fundamental factor of our culture is that everybody counts. Everybody has a voice.

Even if you have a hierarchy, you can still foster the mentality that everybody counts by participating in philanthropy with your team and continually asking them how you can help them.

When employees feel you have their back, they'll give more to you. My team deeply values that I've never laid anybody off and that I put people ahead of profits, especially if they have worked in other agencies and either been laid off or seen their friends get laid off. Saying as a company that we'll stand by you through the bad times and that we don't look at you as an asset on a spreadsheet creates a real camaraderie—we're in this together.

Even if you are not in a position to institute a no-layoffs policy, you still have the ability as a leader of a team to show your people you care about them. Taking an interest in their lives, celebrating their successes, and supporting them when they struggle goes a long way toward building the trust that serves as a backbone for a great relationship.

CHAPTER SEVEN

TENETS OF EMPATHETIC LEADERSHIP

For a positive culture to flourish, managers from the top down need to lead with empathy, not intimidation. In this chapter, I will share my principles for being an empathetic leader so that you have a practical guide for how to instill a positive culture among your team.

ELEVATE THE TOP 10 PERCENT INSTEAD OF ELIMINATING THE BOTTOM 10 PERCENT

There's a common business practice to rank employees against each other and terminate the bottom 10 percent of performers each year. Companies that do this think it will strengthen the organization, but in practice, it's disruptive and demotivating to the team (not to mention incredibly callous). Arbitrarily ranking people against each other causes uneasiness throughout the company. If your employees see people get let go who may not be superstars but who show up and contribute, they will begin to feel uneasy, and it will create tension within the organization.

If you do a good job hiring, training, and nurturing the company's culture, your bottom 10 percent shouldn't be poor performers. In fact, they may be better than the top 50 percent of employees at another business. If your bottom 10 percent is so damaging to your organization that they need to be cut each year, it's more important for you as a leader to look in the mirror, because you're not recruiting the right people, not training them well, or not treating them properly.

Rather than trying to get rid of those perceived weak links, focus on *elevating* the superstars in your company who will take you to the next level. At Fingerpaint, we pay extra attention to developing and uplifting our top 20 percent of performers. For example, we identified an exceptional employee with amazing leadership potential in our Saratoga office, but we didn't have the opportunities in that office at that time to best develop her in her career. So we created a position for her in our New Jersey office that will provide her with additional responsibility along with management and leadership training so that she can grow within Fingerpaint.

The path to success for an empathetic leader is to identify your superstars and do everything you can to empower them to contribute more to the organization.

TREAT YOUR STAFF LIKE FAMILY

Most of us spend more time with our coworkers than our actual families. For a leader, it's important to treat your staff as human beings whom you care about, not just as employees who work for you. Be attentive to their needs, and try to help them when they need it, just as you would with a family member.

To me, treating employees like family means that you feel a responsibility to them and you care for them more deeply than a typical boss-employee relationship. You're there for them when they need you. In addition to being a boss, you're almost like a parent to your people. Even if some of them are older than you, you should make sure they feel taken care of and relieve their stress whenever you can so that they can thrive. It will make your company stronger.

When one of our employees in Pennsylvania lost his father, the leader of the office drove two hours each way to show his support at the wake. For someone running an entire office, that is very uncommon, but we have a culture that our people care for each other in a substantial human way.

We had an employee who was moving from an apartment to her new house with her husband and young child, and their landlord was charging them an exorbitant cancellation fee. They were going to hire a lawyer, and it was going to cause them a lot of angst. She was a relatively new employee, and I wanted to show her that we'd take care of her, so we paid the fee so that she could focus on work and not have to deal with that stress.

If people see that you care about them as people, and they know that you won't just use them as an employee, that tends to come back in spades. They work harder. They're more loyal. The success of your business rises and falls based on them, so the more invested they are in the company, the better for everyone.

SHOW INTEREST IN YOUR PEOPLE AT EVERY LEVEL OF THE COMPANY

Make an effort to show as much interest in the lives of the cleaning staff as you do with the top-level managers. If every level of the company sees the boss as a good person who cares about everyone and not just the people driving the bottom line, it creates a compassionate and friendly environment that people want to be in.

I want people to be able to approach me and feel that I'm here for them regardless of their level as opposed to people getting nervous when I walk down the hall because they're worried that I'll judge them.

A major reason we don't have titles at Fingerpaint is so that everyone treats each other with respect, which tends to create a culture that people find very appealing. This has absolutely helped us with recruiting because our younger employees, who have felt the sting of being on the bottom of the food chain at other companies, love to share that people treat each other well here, even at the entry level.

NEVER RAISE YOUR VOICE TO EMPLOYEES

I do not yell at employees. I've fired managers in the past who have led with intimidation or fear. Fear is completely counterintuitive to doing great work. Yelling makes everyone less comfortable, which leads to mistakes. People will feel like they're on pins and needles if their boss yells at them, and I don't want our people to ever be in that kind of environment. Yelling also demonstrates that you are losing control as a leader.

As a leader in the company, you have to set the tone. When mistakes happen, I use a little bit of sarcasm and laughter to defuse the situation but still get my message across, or I simply explain respectfully what the mistake was and why we can't repeat it.

We have had a situation in which an editor missed a grammar mistake, and we had to pay $10,000 for a reprint. Of course, I need to tell them we need to do better, but at the same time, I have to do it in a respectful way that assures them that they're not going to lose their job over it and discuss how we can create checks and balances to ensure it doesn't happen again, because we can't afford those mistakes.

One of our junior people fell victim to an email scam in which someone posed as me asking her to buy and email iTunes gift cards. When someone pointed it out to me, I'm sure she was terrified that she'd lose her job. Instead of giving her a hard time or waiting for her to apologize, I proactively went to her and said, "We've all been victims to these types of scams. Just triple-check next time if something looks suspicious. But please don't lose sleep over this. It happens." She knows to be sharper about it going forward and didn't feel terrible coming into the office the next day.

DON'T TAKE YOURSELF TOO SERIOUSLY

When leaders are self-effacing or make fun of themselves in public or in front of the staff, it puts everyone at ease. Your staff will see that you have a sense of humor and don't think you're the smartest person in the room. People want to work for someone who doesn't take themselves too seriously. Being funny and lighthearted helps employees relax and be themselves.

At staff meetings I make jokes at my own expense in a way that props other people up. I want them to know that I understand that they're better at some things than I am, and I don't see myself as a supreme leader who is God's gift to advertising.

I'll find somebody in the audience at a meeting whom I know is an absolutely expert about something and joke that I know *way* more than they do about their area of expertise. It's so blatantly obvious I'm joking that people laugh, and it reminds them that I know their value, I respect them, and I am aware that I don't know everything.

Showing your sense of humor, especially at your own expense, creates a comfortable atmosphere that people can do their best work in.

REMEMBER WHAT IT FEELS LIKE TO HAVE PRESSURE TO MAKE RENT

As people start making money and having success in leadership positions, they may forget what it feels like to have financial and career pressures. To relate to your employees, it's important to have empathy for their stresses.

I remember what it was like when I had my first job. I was bringing home $600 a month, but my rent was $330, and I had a student loan payment of $113. I remember not being able to afford a car and a telephone. It's part of growing up and part of life. When I speak to people starting out in their careers or making a career transition, I remind myself of that.

I remember what it's like to have the day-to-day stress of finances and having young kids and student loans and making rent. Sharing your understanding with staff will go a long way toward letting them feel that you understand them and care about what they go through.

NEVER LET PEOPLE SEE YOU SWEAT

It may be cliché, but when the chips are down, it's the leader's responsibility to be the voice of optimism—to let people know that we are in it together, and we will succeed together. In the early days of Fingerpaint, when we lost a major client and were struggling to survive, I remember being afraid we weren't going to make it. But I made a concerted effort to be the voice of optimism and project confidence that everything would work out.

I don't mean that you should hide important information from your staff. Transparency is vital to your success. My employees knew that we had lost a lot of revenue, and I shared that news with them. But they saw that my reaction to the struggle was to rally everyone together, to not lay anyone off, and to forge ahead with confidence. If I had said, "I'm really worried, and I don't know how I'm going to handle this," the staff would not have coped well.

When people see their leader stressed out, they panic. When you face challenges as a leader, you have to solve them in private and not transfer that worry to your staff.

Bill McEllen, a senior leader in our company overseeing both our New York and New Jersey offices, is an expert at leading people through some tough times, and he summed up a recent experience in this regard very well.

"In the health-care marketing space, when products don't get approved by the FDA, or a company stops promoting their medications, it can cause enormous issues.

"Both of those things happened in our New York office during the fourth quarter last year. Between Mallinckrodt's stannsoporfin FDA rejection and Avadel stopping promotion of Noctiva, we unexpectedly, and without fault, lost 30 percent of our business. To say we had to act quickly to keep up morale and save people's jobs was an understatement.

"Thirty percent business loss in a quarter for most (if not all) agencies would mean immediate job loss and could put a company into a death spiral. However, with immediate and transparent communication, rallying around teams, reassigning people, and quickly going after new business, we were able to stabilize things in short order."

In that situation, there was certainly an opportunity to panic, but Bill remained steady in choppy waters and rallied the people behind him, and we were able to right the ship.

DON'T BE AFRAID TO SHARE BAD NEWS. PEOPLE WANT TRANSPARENCY.

While you shouldn't show emotional stress, which is a response to difficult challenges, it is important to share both good and bad news with your people. If we lose a piece of business or a pitch or if we're up for an award and we don't get it, it's important for people to hear about it from us and for us to recognize that it's not the end of the world. We'll get through it. This is how we'll adjust to get better.

You have to bring people together when things are bad and be transparent with them so that they're not worried that you're concealing things. My experience has been that people want honesty. If you're in a rough patch, and you tell your people that bonuses will be tight or that you cannot give raises because of X, Y, or Z, there will be less fallout than just cutting raises without explanation. If you share your reasons for things that are disappointing, your employees are much more apt to give you the benefit of the doubt. But if you shield them from bad news, and then their raises are not as high as they expected or bonuses are cut, people will think you're hoarding money for yourself.

REACT FAST WHEN MATTERS NEED TO BE FIXED

There will be problems. You will make mistakes. It's important that you are approachable and that when people come to you with a problem, you react fast to fix it or at least to explore solutions. As mentioned in a prior chapter, I was informed by several of our pregnant employees that our maternity and paternity leave policy was unacceptable. Within two days, we dramatically improved it.

Of course, you will not be able to fix everything, but you have to listen to your staff's concerns and value their input. If you can't change something, explain to them why not. They may not agree with you, but they will appreciate that you cared enough to listen, explore it, and share your reasoning.

DON'T DRINK YOUR OWN KOOL-AID

Don't believe that you are the best thing since the wheel. Embrace greatness in your field, even if it comes from others. People are often quick to dismiss other competitors' success, especially in advertising, which is a very cutthroat, ego-driven industry. I've always taken the position that we need to acknowledge that there are many health-care advertising agencies that produce great work, or they wouldn't be in business.

If we lose a client or a pitch, it's easy to make excuses for ourselves. "Their decision maker was friends with our competitor; of course they went with them." That might make us feel better, but it does not help us understand how we can be better next time.

If somebody wins business instead of you or does better in the market than you, they probably deserved to beat you. They brought it better than you did. And that's OK. There's no sense in bashing them. Instead, realize that you can use the good work that others create to motivate you and teach you to do better. What did they do better than you? Where can you improve for next time? Having the self-awareness and dignity to be able to accept that goes a long way toward making your team better.

Dumping on your competition makes you look insecure, and that negativity can pervade your organization and harm your culture. Plus, your future employees may come from your competitors, so imagine how they will feel if they know you trashed them before they joined you.

MAKE PHILANTHROPY A CORNERSTONE OF YOUR BUSINESS

You should not do charity work because you feel that you are required to; do it because it feels great to help others. As we've covered throughout the book, people want to work for a company that cares about making a positive difference in the world. If you can engage your employees to share causes that they care about and then support their contributions to those causes, they will feel even more positive about your company and work that much harder for you.

WHEN HIRING, FOCUS ON CHARACTER RATHER THAN ACCOMPLISHMENTS

A person's character will tell you more about how they will be as an employee than any point of pride they have on a resume. When hiring entry-level employees, don't focus on the prestige of their school or their GPA. No one is ever qualified to do anything when they graduate, including me. Entry-level employees essentially come with a clean slate.

I had a 2.8 GPA at Syracuse. While that's a good school, I certainly wasn't a Rhodes Scholar. Now I run a 350-plus-person company. I meet successful business owners and sharp executives every day who didn't graduate summa cum laude. Business is a completely different skill set than school. It takes teamwork, passion, work ethic, people skills, and confidence.

I tell our leaders to find people who are passionate and take on projects in their communities that show teamwork; people who seem hungry, energetic, and authentic; and people who have done their research before coming into an interview and who will be team players. A GPA can tell you someone's academic chops, but if they're afraid of their own shadow, how will they ever be able to work on a team?

The same rule applies for hiring experienced people. Don't just look at where they worked or what their titles were. What reputation do they have among peers and subordinates? Are they easy to work with? Or are they talented but so negative that they grate on those around them?

Even people with twenty years of experience need to have the same (or stronger) people skills as an entry-level worker to work well on the team. Hiring based on qualifications instead of character is a quick way to destroy your team's chemistry.

AGREE TO TAKE MEETINGS FROM STUDENTS

Whenever I get a call from a kid at Syracuse or a high school student who wants to meet with me and ask me about marketing, I always accept the meeting. It takes tremendous courage for someone that age to blindly call someone they respect, so I want to reward that and give them some guidance. I certainly didn't have that kind of moxie when I was a kid.

It is an honor to be able to share your knowledge with the next generation. And who knows—that kid may come work for you a few years down the road and be a valuable contributor.

ACCEPT THAT EMPLOYEES WON'T CARE AS MUCH AS YOU

Fingerpaint is one of the most important parts of my life. It is my family's nest egg. It is the culmination of all my work and personal experiences. Fingerpaint allows me to employ hundreds of wonderful people, provide them with health care, and give them an opportunity to take care of their families. It provides me with the means to make a positive impact in my community. It's a very big part of my life.

But the company doesn't have that same level of importance for the people who work there. It's important that I recognize that and do not expect my employees to have the same level of passion and accountability that I have.

You need to be mindful of what is important to your people if you're going to build a culture of empathy.

The majority of people who work for you do so to earn the means to support their lives outside of work. Even if you simply run a department and don't own your company, understand that for most of your employees, the success of your mission is not their life's passion.

They have different needs and values. It doesn't mean that they're not going to be great workers and wonderful people, but at the end of the day, their own career and life satisfaction comes first for them. They value opportunities for growth, their home life, their children, and other things.

You need to be mindful of what is important to your people if you're going to build a culture of empathy. If work forces people to consistently have to miss Little League games, dance recitals, and parents' anniversary parties, then you haven't built a culture that values what matters to your employees. That's not being an empathetic leader.

Often you see companies take the approach that everyone has to get in line with the same drive as the leader, but that simply isn't realistic. Many consulting firms build a culture that burns people out for the first few years that they're there, and if they make it through that hazing period, the company will promote them to a management or partnership position. Some companies have actual leaflets they hand out at job interviews about what prospective employees' spouses could expect if they work there—missed dinners, weekend work, and so on.

I've always thought that was ridiculous. You're going to drain your people. You'll have people willing to climb over anybody else's body to get ahead. It creates an unhealthy, adversarial working relationship that is not productive.

Work is hard. Life is hard. By treating your employees as people first and recognizing what is important to them outside of work, you will find great long-term contributors to your organization who will look out for each other.

APPROACH PERFORMANCE WITH GUIDANCE, NOT INTIMIDATION

If someone isn't performing as well as you expect, look for ways to help before considering letting them go. The way I see it, we hired the person, so if it is not working out, that's at least partially on us. We owe that person to do all we can to enable them to be successful, as long as we see effort and good teamwork on their part. I know how hard it is for people to change jobs or go without pay for several months, so when there are performance issues, I try very hard to help them improve to the level that we expect from them, rather than simply cutting them at the first sign of a problem.

If people are slipping, it's incumbent upon us to make sure that they're aware of the issue and that it doesn't just come up every six months at a performance review. We consistently need to talk through it and search for ways to guide them to be better. If I can see that someone is making an effort, I can give them the benefit of the doubt that unforeseen circumstances may be causing them to falter. What we cannot accept is people not being good team players and not helping their coworkers out.

Unfortunately, sometimes every leader needs to let people go, but rather than putting pressure on people with the fear that they may lose their jobs, an empathetic leader looks for ways to help willing workers improve before considering termination.

ASK, "HOW CAN I HELP?"

Asking employees how you can help when they are struggling is extremely powerful. You never know what they're going through or what they need unless you ask. We've had people struggle while going through a divorce, and we helped recommend counselors. We've helped employees with substance abuse issues get treatment. A lot of roles at our company require travel, but we do everything we can to accommodate when people cannot travel due to issues at home, such as having a sick parent to take care of or a young child.

By looking for ways to help our employees when they need it, we build a stronger relationship with them that builds loyalty to the company and a culture of caring for each other that positively affects everyone in the company and all our clients.

RESPECT YOUR EMPLOYEES' CAREER GOALS

Empower your people to achieve the career paths that they choose instead of steering them down a career path that you envision. Some companies have rigid career progressions, and if someone does not want to follow that path, eventually they are shown the door.

We've had great employees whom we wanted to promote but who wanted to stay in the jobs they had. Maybe they aren't motivated by money, or they have kids at home and it's more important for them to spend time with their families than to get a promotion that may require more travel. We understand that and respect having valued performers who are happy and productive in their roles as opposed to saying, "This guy doesn't have what it takes to grow within the company; let's cut him loose."

As a result, we end up with great performers at all levels of the company who are happy to be in their roles.

STRIVE TO MAKE PEOPLE'S LIVES BETTER

Life is hard, so we try to remember that work serves life, not the other way around. Kids and pets are always welcome in our offices, so people do not have to worry about finding a sitter or being away from their furry friends.

If someone has a lot going on at home and needs to work from home for a while, we accommodate that. I bought a building down the street from our office with four apartments specifically for our staff to use if they have to work late and don't want to drive home, or if there's bad weather, or if they went out after work and don't want to drink and drive.

I try to do whatever I can to help my people. One of our employees had to fly to Florida last minute because their parent suddenly fell ill. Because it was so last minute, the flight was going to cost $2,000. I heard about it and used my airline miles to get them a flight so they didn't have to pay the massive last-minute fee.

If you can continually work to understand the stresses that your employees face and do what you can to reduce them, you're well on your way to leading with empathy.

CELEBRATE SUCCESSES

Find reasons to acknowledge the great things your team does. Most companies don't celebrate enough. If they do celebrate, they do it in small groups, or the leadership team goes out for drinks but doesn't include the staff.

In all our offices, we have a bell that we ring whenever there's good news, and we all gather together and celebrate collectively as a team. Of course, we don't consider simply doing our jobs bell worthy. But if we just won or expanded a deal, or were nominated for awards, or announced that we're opening a new office, we come together and celebrate.

It makes a big impact on your staff to feel that they are part of a team that is having success. When you do accomplish something important, celebrate with them and share the credit and good feelings.

* * *

By leading with empathy, you can continually nurture a positive culture that will lead to happy workers producing for your business.

CHAPTER EIGHT

WHY GREAT CULTURES GO BAD AND WHAT TO DO TO PREVENT IT

A positive culture can take years to build but just moments to disintegrate.

While I was running my first advertising agency, Palio, I put in a ton of effort to foster an empathetic company culture. Although it was before the days of Glassdoor and social media business reviews, we had a great reputation in the industry. People loved working at Palio; we had very little turnover, and applicants from larger, more bureaucratic companies constantly sought us out to work for us. The company was thriving, growing 20 to 30 percent each year, eventually becoming a $25 million-a-year agency.

In 2006, my investors and I decided to sell Palio and its sister companies to a large corporation. I stayed on for twenty-four months through the transition but quickly realized that I was more suited to run an independent company where I could call the shots and not have to answer to shareholders or a board of directors.

In 2008, my transition period was over, and I left to start Fingerpaint on a card table in a four-hundred-square-foot office. As of today, we have grown to a market capitalization of over $170 million.

However, as Fingerpaint grew, Palio crumbled. Within a few short years, the company that purchased Palio closed the business. What was recently a growing high-octane $25 million agency with a fantastic reputation was shuttered.

So what went wrong?

The culture changed, and as the theme of this book has shown, a company's culture defines the work it produces. Once I left, it took a remarkably short amount of time for Palio's culture to fall apart. Layoffs occurred for the first time. Employees and clients fled for other agencies. Put simply, once the culture changed, good people left, and the work suffered. Pretty soon, there was nothing left to salvage.

This story is quite common among mergers and acquisitions. *Harvard Business Review* published a piece on the devastation that clashing company cultures can inflict on mergers.

It defined two types of cultures: "Tight company cultures value consistency and routine ... and use strict rules and processes." They have "an efficient orderliness and reassuring predictability, but are less adaptable." Meanwhile, "loose cultures tend to be open and creative, but are more disorganized."

After studying more than 4,500 mergers spanning multiple decades and continents, the researchers found that when one company acquired another with the opposite type of culture, there was a decrease in assets of $200 million in net income per year from the acquisition's value. If the culture divide was markedly pronounced, that yearly income dropped by over $600 million.[1]

---

1 Michele Gelfand et al., "One Reason Mergers Fail: The Two Cultures Aren't Compatible," *Harvard Business Review*, October 2, 2018, https://hbr.org/2018/10/one-reason-mergers-fail-the-two-cultures-arent-compatible.

Those numbers represent customers being unhappy with the change in work product as a result of the company culture change and voting with their wallets to stay away.

Most clients of ad agencies don't see the connection between a healthy agency culture and the work that they receive. They don't see that a positive culture creatively inspires people to produce better work or that it ensures that the agency employees treat clients the same way that they're used to being treated. Because of our culture at Fingerpaint, we become almost family to our clients. They love working with us because we treat them better, in large part because we treat each other better.

On the other hand, when harsh bosses lead their agencies with intimidation, that roughness translates into how their people relate to their customers. It creates contentious relationships that are unpleasant and produces worse work for the customers.

There are several reasons a great culture can go south, whether it's in the agency world or at any organization. Here are the main reasons and some tips you can use to stem the tide if you notice the culture at your company taking a downturn.

A new leader arrives and stops upholding the company values.
A change in leadership is a major inflection point. If a new leader does not absorb and uphold the values of the company they come into, the culture can disintegrate. So often I see companies with really healthy cultures get acquired or have a change in leadership, and the company completely falls apart.

Employees will say, "The heartbeat got ripped out of the place." Massive changes occur, and the staff feels that suddenly their workplace is no longer a place where management cares about them. They feel that they are in an environment revolving around money that treats them like a number. At that point, everyone looks out for themselves and not for each other or the company. Good people start heading for the doors, and before you know it, everyone left is looking around asking, "Why did everything go south? We were a great company."

> You can't set and forget a positive culture or work on it only every once in a while. You have to consistently care about your staff and lead with empathy.

If you are in a position to be a new leader at a company or a leader of a department that was recently merged with yours, ensure that you take the time to understand the employees' values and show your new people that you care about them.

Even without a change in leadership, the same effect can happen if leadership takes their eye off of the ball and forgets that the staff's hard work is what butters their bread. It doesn't take long for a pronounced negative change to occur. If I come into the office at Fingerpaint tomorrow and start treating profit as the top priority, or if I change my personality and become more aggressive with people, or God forbid if I have to lay anybody off, then suddenly the aura of compassion and empathy that we've built over more than a decade can collapse.

You can't set and forget a positive culture or work on it only every once in a while. You have to consistently care about your staff and lead with empathy. If you as an existing leader forget to take care of your people, it can be just as damaging to your company's culture as a new leader coming in and making changes.

The company has layoffs or a rash of firings.

Layoffs and firings destroy morale. When people see good contributors let go, they worry for their own jobs. When their friends get fired, they feel the brunt of it. Everyone starts walking on eggshells when they're at work and looking for an escape plan when they're off work. Layoffs or firings should not be systematic—they should be done only if absolutely necessary. They harm your culture more than they help the bottom line.

Everyone gets burned out from an exceedingly high workload.

We honestly struggle with high workload at Fingerpaint. It's the biggest strain on our culture and the biggest challenge facing our leadership team. We're a growing company, and we often can't hire people fast enough to keep up with the business we bring in. When clients expand their business and we win a few pitches, before we know it, we have fifty open jobs. Of course, it's important to hire selectively and bring people on who will be positive for the company, but in the meantime, that work burden falls to the existing staff.

When you're leading a growing business, you constantly work to bring people on as quickly as possible, but hiring simply takes time. Recruiting, onboarding, and training is a process. As a result, when there's extra work, even if we begin the hiring process immediately, it takes time before new people can relieve the burden. So until I can get new staff onboarded and trained, the work gets absorbed by folks in the company who already have full plates.

It's OK for a little while, but if it takes six or eight weeks to hire people, it becomes a real stress point. The staff may feel that the leadership team is blind to it and that if they work sixty hours a week, the owners don't care because they're making money.

Maybe some business owners feel that way, but I hate when our people are overworked. It makes me feel that I'm failing as a leader because I'm taking our people away from their families. I cringe every time I get a group email at seven o'clock at night saying, "I'm ordering dinner. Any requests?" because it means that people who are working for me are not having dinner at home. To me it serves as a reminder that I need to do better.

Despite my efforts to make the staff feel appreciated by providing job security, health care, sabbaticals, and spot bonuses, if they've been working late and haven't seen their family in six weeks, they have to question, "What am I doing there? I can't live like this." I don't want them to live like that either. We can lose good people because they feel like they can't have a life outside of work. Fortunately, it is rare for us to lose employees, but 99 percent of the time when people leave Fingerpaint, they do so because they feel burned out.

Burnout is common in the advertising industry, because advertising tends to attract type A workers. Most people who have worked in advertising and choose to work for a successful growing business expect to work hard. But there is a misconception that in a healthy culture, they should be overworked. They should not. It's one thing if they need to stay late for a week here and there to finish up a big project. But if there are sustained long hours, week after week, the staff tends to feel that either I'm oblivious or I don't care.

It's a very challenging aspect of our business. One thing that goes hand in hand with our no-layoff policy is that I cannot have an excess capacity of people with no work to do, because suddenly we can become upside down financially. If I'm running a good company, I can't have people sitting on the bench just waiting for a win. The other side of that is if we win a $5 million account, it takes twenty-five full-time people to serve that account. Some of those people will be on the existing team, but every new client we bring in means we need to hire new people.

It's a very difficult scale to balance; on one side, we have amazing benefits, great pay, strong camaraderie, and no layoffs, but on the other side, we have to make money to pay the bills. One of the reasons we have all of these great benefits and give out surprise spot bonuses is because we recognize that advertising is not an easy business.

High workload isn't a problem that is solvable overnight, but we are working to ease that burden by building a pipeline of candidates to shorten the hiring process, with a combination of recruiting and dialing up our social media presence so that people can get a sense for what we're all about.

Last year, I spent $700,000 on recruiters. That's a lot when you're a $60 million company. I'm not looking to pull that $700,000 out of the business. I'm happy with what I make. I live on a wonderful farm with goats, chickens, dogs, and cats. I want to create a place that's great for people, and if we have an extra $700,000, I'm going to give additional benefits and bonuses and maybe add another philanthropic project.

We try to get everybody to recognize there's no magic bullet to recruiting; it's a team effort. We ask the staff to be minirecruiters in a way, to keep an eye out for whom they know in the industry that we may want to bring over. Culturally, who would be a good fit? Who is unhappy with their current employer and is a rock star?

We encourage our employees to write Glassdoor reviews about us. We don't tell them to be positive or negative, but we want people to share what it's like to work here because the more that people outside the company know about us, the faster we can bring in quality candidates to ease the burden on our existing staff.

However, even when we have a strong pipeline of people clamoring to join us, it still takes time to bring them in. If they're doing freelance work, they have to finish it. If they're with another company, they have to give notice to their employer. Hiring takes time for everybody—not just us.

I tell people at Fingerpaint that we will chase work-life balance relentlessly knowing that we will never catch it. We'll do the best we can. I also can't legislate it. I can't send an email out saying, "From now on, we'll all have work-life balance." We have to monitor ourselves, knowing that I am never going to punish someone for rescheduling a meeting with me because they have a parent-teacher conference.

We have to cover for each other. I tell our staff, "If you need to get the hell out of here for something, get the hell out of here. Push back on clients if you have to. If business is slow for a week, leave at noon. I have no problem with that. Because I guarantee you, it will pick up again, so take advantage of the time when you have it."

But our people are so dedicated, and I think they really do care for me and the leadership team, which makes them want to try harder. Most of the time we have to save them from themselves, because they're so committed, which I love. That's why I'm so proud of our sabbatical program, because it really does save us from ourselves. There's no email, no cell phone, no work. It's so therapeutic. Imagine taking a month off and getting paid to do whatever you want. It's life changing for the type A workers who flock to our business.

In any growing business, there will be times that people are over-worked. But if you see that high workload becomes a stress point for your business, do all that you can to ease the burden on your staff and to show appreciation for their hard work. Communicate to them that you are aware of the problem and are taking steps to fix it, and reward them for their extra effort. It's important to do what you can to reduce burnout, because workload can absolutely erode your culture and cost you good people.

Company celebrations or team-building activities are significantly diminished.

Celebrating success as a group is extremely important for maintaining a positive culture. Executives going out to celebrate without the staff doesn't cut it. Everyone needs to share in the company's success.

In 2018, I flew every single one of our employees out to the JW Marriott resort in Scottsdale, Arizona, for four days to celebrate a decade of putting people first at Fingerpaint. We recognized exceptional employees and did team-building events and fun group activities like horseback riding and mountain biking.

We pair many of our team-building exercises with philanthropy, so everyone can come together and feel good about working to make a difference in the community. In 2017, we raised money for Together We Rise, an organization that helps foster kids. We closed Fingerpaint for the day, and the team created bags for kids, dubbed "sweet cases," that included hygiene kits, teddy bears, blankets, coloring books, and crayons. We built bikes to donate as well and raised money for the cause.

The following year, we once again closed shop for the day, and we all got together for Operation Lunch Lady to create meals for kids who don't have enough to eat during the summer. In one day, we packed sixty-five thousand meals! Participating in positive activities together as a company creates a feeling of goodwill within our staff and a bond between them that tightens our group together.

If you see that there haven't been many celebrations or team-building activities lately, don't take it lightly. Find a way to bring the staff together around a positive event or activity, and your culture will thank you for it.

Your company stops working on philanthropic endeavors.

Now more than ever, people want to work for companies that they feel are making a positive impact in the world. However, advertising tends to be an industry that is self-serving, almost like banking. People work at investment banks because they know that banks are in the business to make money. To a banker looking at a spreadsheet, philanthropy is purely a cost. Many advertising firms see it the same way. It's very easy for someone making a budget to say, "We're going to increase our margin by 3 percent by getting rid of philanthropy."

But doing so is devastating to the culture. It dehumanizes the company and makes people less proud of where they work. If I were a betting man, I'd wager that the 3 percent margin gained by cutting philanthropy is not worth the losses that you will feel within the company culture.

The flip side where we can get into trouble is asking people to do philanthropic work when they're already overworked. If someone is working sixty hours a week, and I tell them we found a great cause to do some free work for, they probably will not be thrilled.

For instance, we've done marketing programs to raise money to fund a clinic for the traveling workers at the racetrack in Saratoga. Many of them barely speak English, they're working themselves to the bone and shipping money back home, and they don't even have health care. I've donated money to the cause, and we have a whole team of people working on this program to raise more money to ensure that they receive health care.

That makes our people feel great—as long as they are not overworked. I don't want them to say, "I haven't been home a single night for dinner this week, and now you expect me to get fired up to work on this?"

It's a double-edged sword that we balance by shifting work among the team. Because we have four offices, we can shift the philanthropic work around based on level of busyness. We can plug in projects to offices that are a bit slower as opposed to overburdening an office that's at capacity, and because the projects are pro bono, the non profit beneficiaries are usually accommodating. If we have to delay a project, they're usually fine with it as long as we communicate with them, because they know that we're working pro bono and that we do care about their cause.

While it may not always be easy to make philanthropy a priority, it is important that your team feels that their company makes the world a better place.

ACCEPT THAT NOT EVERYONE WILL BE HAPPY

Keeping in mind that the above five stresses can damage your culture, it's important to remember that even in a good company, there will be problems. Despite all your best intentions and all the things that leadership can do, there will always be some people who are disgruntled.

Recently I spent close to $300,000 to provide a spot bonus of $1,000 to every Fingerpaint employee to thank them for winning a major industry award. I sent a video to the entire staff and said, "I know $1,000 doesn't mean you can buy a new car or a new house, but hopefully you can spend a weekend away with your family or friends or pay down some student loans. Whatever you choose, this a token of our gratitude, and hopefully it'll help." I received a ton of grateful responses from the staff, but I guarantee you that some people felt, "I worked the last three weekends; of course I should get a bonus."

I've found that if I do the best I can and it's not good enough for certain people, that's OK. I know that no other agency will care for them as much as we do. If they're still unhappy, most of the time it's because advertising is not a good fit for them. Having a positive culture does not mean that everyone is happy 100 percent of the time. It means that more often than not, people take care of each other.

ACKNOWLEDGE THAT YOU ARE NOT PERFECT

Accepting that people will sometimes be unhappy doesn't mean that you can do no wrong or let yourself off the hook for mistakes that you make. Sometimes people are unhappy because I and my leadership team failed. Maybe it took us too long to get people on board after we won too much business. Perhaps we didn't realize how hard someone was working on a project and did not reward them appropriately. But you do the best you can.

My overarching philosophy is that people will usually recognize when you try to help them. For the most part, they know that we don't bring in work just to squeeze money out of them. They know that we do it because we want to grow the business and pump opportunities back to the employees.

Most of your employees will give you the benefit of the doubt when they recognize that you're empathetic, that you care about the community and about them, and that you are not just trying to raise the share price or fatten your wallet.

I try very hard to have a good pulse on the staff, but I can't know what's going on in every employee's life. I rely on my leadership team to keep track of everybody and take care of them by giving them comp time if they need it or rewarding them with spot awards or little gestures. You do the best you can, but there will be times you falter. If you can show empathy and act as an empathetic leader, on balance, you should still have a strong culture, even if there are hits from time to time.

CHAPTER NINE

HOW TO MEASURE AND IMPROVE PERFORMANCE

Most companies evaluate their agencies on a regular basis, such as quarterly or yearly. However, very few companies provide their agencies with a formal opportunity to evaluate them, which is vital to continued growth. Evaluation in a relationship is most beneficial as a two-way street.

The agency is responsible for producing high-quality work that is on strategy, listening to the client, and delivering on time and on budget. However, the client has responsibilities as well: to provide necessary information to their agency, to be accessible to answer questions, to provide timely feedback, and to commit to a consistent strategy rather than continually changing focus. If either side is not accountable for their responsibilities, the relationship will fail. That's why it's important to come together in a formal setting once a quarter and review the ups and downs on both sides.

MUTUAL EVALUATION OF THE RELATIONSHIP

While it's easy for you to evaluate the agency's strengths and weaknesses, asking them to measure you in the same areas can provide incredible benefits to your team, help you find areas where the relationship isn't functioning optimally, and uncover opportunities to improve on both sides.

Both sides should look for strengths that they can double down on and look to fix gaps in communication that may be causing performance issues. For example, you can evaluate if the agency is providing account leadership, if they are accountable to the budget and deadlines, and if they are taking your feedback and effectively implementing it.

The agency can also share if your team is treating its team as partners by giving them all necessary information, providing feedback, and answering questions in a timely fashion. Is your team accurately communicating deadlines, proactively sharing relevant news as it becomes available, and being inclusive in general?

The agency needs to communicate clearly and concisely. Is it informing the client when a project gets off schedule or if it's running into a budget issue? Is it consistently in communication while at the same time recognizing that it has to be mindful of the client's time?

The client must give the agency all necessary information and provide access to the various departments that the agency needs to access to do its job appropriately, such as medical, regulatory, legal, sales, and managed care teams. The client also should share both positive and negative feedback on work consistently for the agency to clearly understand what it's looking for.

Both sides should evaluate how well the other is communicating and look to iron out issues in communication, because that can save both sides time and money and lead to a much healthier relationship.

For each area of the business that you hope to evaluate, it is vital for both sides to measure each other. For instance, if you want to gauge the effectiveness of your agency's delivery on strategy, it's not enough to note if the agency is providing sound strategic ideas to you that will differentiate the product and uphold a consistent strategy to make an impact in the market. You also need to hear the agency's perspective on your own team's openness to selecting a strategy and sticking with it.

One common pitfall in this regard is if a client overvalues ad-testing results. Before going to market, we test the creative material with certain groups, such as physicians, nurses, and patients. However, during testing, doctors generally overrate creative work that feels familiar to them.

If a client is not willing to trust a bold strategy to differentiate themselves in the marketplace because testing shows that doctors like something more traditional, they'll end up with more of the same. That's why you see so many nearly identical health-care ads on TV—couples strolling with big smiles, parents swinging their kids around, children running through a field or a park. Those ads test well because doctors are used to seeing them. But there's a big difference between testing well and being memorable. For creative to make an impact in the market, it has to be memorable, not just comfortable. Resist sameness just because it tests well.

For real performance growth for your brand, you cannot expect to simply evaluate the agency's performance—you have to allow it to evaluate yours as well. Otherwise, you may find that switching to a new agency leads to the same issues you had with the past one, because there will be blind spots within your own team that hold back performance.

ESTABLISH A FORMAL REVIEW SCHEDULE AND PROCESS

The value of a formal check-in cannot be overstated. Obviously, there are a lot of dynamics in play in a client-agency relationship. There are human beings on both sides who make mistakes and ever-changing markets and goals. A system for evaluating performance is needed for both sides to be able to step out of the chaos of day-to-day operations and methodically take stock of what is and is not working.

You should have an idea of key areas that you want to measure regularly with your agency. Some examples might be innovation, strategy, communication, account management, timeline and budget management, and culture.

A quarterly review also provides a forum for people to give difficult feedback, which some people, myself included, may have a tough time giving face to face in the course of every workday.

Not only does the review help us improve at key areas; it also gives both sides a clear set of expectations so we can measure each other's concerns at regular intervals and ask, Have we addressed it? Are we moving in the right direction? That yardstick is important for the growth of the relationship. There's nothing worse for an agency than getting this call out of the blue—"We're not happy. We're switching agencies"—when the agency was unaware of the issues the client had and did not have a chance to address them.

Of course, it's not pleasant for a client to receive the same message. We've had to fire clients because they were brutal to work with. You try to communicate about issues in the course of work, but that is often ineffective. By putting a regular review process in place, you can identify issues and get the ship moving in the right direction.

Often during this evaluation process, we find that the senior leaders on either side may not even be aware of problems that are occurring in the day-to-day operations. If a vice president of marketing sees that their agency is not hitting deadlines, but they read in the agency's side of the review that their internal team is taking weeks to get back to the agency with necessary information, then they can address that on their end to smooth out the process moving forward. If we hear from the client that our team drops the ball in a certain area, we can address it internally, and both sides have an open path to communicate about these issues going forward.

Many companies do have a formal process for evaluating performance. However, they don't always measure the agency according to the appropriate metrics. In the next sections, I'll address a couple of the common missteps that people make when measuring their agency's performance.

MEASURE WITH A HUMAN EYE, NOT JUST A NUMBERS EYE

Clients are often strictly concerned with, "How is the product performing, and how much am I spending?" Of course, those are important metrics, but there are many other factors that determine if an agency is succeeding or failing.

It's certainly fair to hold the agency accountable for product performance, but the agency is not the sole influence determining a product's success. It could be that managed care is not covering the product. It could be that the sales force is spread too thin, and they're not reaching the right customers. It could be that the market doesn't need the product because there are less expensive options that are equally effective.

In the health-care space, doctors can recognize a product and know all its features and benefits, which is the goal of the agency and the sales force, but still not prescribe it to their patients. When that happens, sometimes there's a problem with the product that no agency can fix. So while an agency should be held accountable for sales performance, there has to be more to an agency evaluation than simply looking at sales.

Much of judging an agency is subjective. There are soft qualities in a relationship that are crucial to success. Is the agency willing to go the extra mile? Does the team come through when you need them? Are they willing to attend research meetings? Will they come to your office if necessary? Are they efficient? Are they strategically bringing ideas that other agencies wouldn't? Are they pushing back when it makes sense to challenge an idea as opposed to just being order takers? Are they proactively coming up with ideas that you haven't thought of? Is the creative breaking through the market? Are they responsive and respectful of your team? These are all the types of questions that clients need to ask themselves when evaluating their agencies.

It goes without saying that the agency has to drive revenue, but if you are not hitting forecasts, and your agency scores well on the aforementioned soft qualities, it's a pretty good indicator that something aside from the agency is preventing you from reaching your numbers, which can help you get to the root of the performance issues.

CONTINUE TO FOSTER A POSITIVE CULTURE

It's important for each side to continually put each other as people first. Agencies need to understand the goals of their clients and honor the trust that the client's marketing team placed in the agency, not only to reach their business goals but their personal career goals as well.

Clients need to show appreciation for their agency partners and recognize that at times, they ask us to pull rabbits out of hats. It's very rare that a client will work all weekend and stay at the office until eleven o'clock at night, but that's not uncommon in the agency world.

Showing appreciation for an agency's effort works wonders for morale, whether that means sending the team food when they're working late, or coming to the agency and taking everybody out to dinner as a thank-you when an important sales milestone is reached, or even sending a simple email to express gratitude when the agency has delivered on a great piece of work.

The clients that put themselves in the agency's shoes and recognize how hard the team has been working are the ones that the agency will really go to battle for. They don't mind working hard if they feel like the clients are good people, and they know that the client isn't going to put pressure on them to work overtime unless absolutely necessary.

The clients that treat their agencies like a printing vendor and crack the whip without any regard for the human aspect of the business will have a completely different experience with the exact same agency. It's very hard for me to motivate people to want to work for those clients. Employees will ask to be taken off accounts with clients that are callous, so ultimately, the client's attitude lowers the quality of their agency team. You'll have turnover on the team, and people will not want to go above and beyond for clients that don't appreciate it.

Show appreciation for your agency as if the people were your own staff. Treat them as a partner to collaborate with, not a vendor to be managed. Lead your agency with transparency, providing all necessary information and access to the various departments that the agency needs to do its job appropriately.

Show appreciation for your agency as if the people were your own staff.

Both sides need to have open communication around timelines and respect each other's needs and processes in this regard. Agencies need to manage their internal resources to make sure that they can get work done on time, which may mean bringing in additional freelancers or using people from other offices to hit a deadline. So to get the best work, clients need to give agencies true deadlines and not fake ones that build in time for missed deadlines.

Be mindful of the fact that the more time an agency has to work on a job, the better the work will be. More time doesn't mean a higher cost—it means that the creative people are going to have more room to kick around ideas, sleep on concepts, and get feedback from each other. Asking, "How much time do you need for this?" goes a long way toward empowering the agency to do its best work.

If the agency asks for extra time on a project, and the deadline is not crucial, extend them that flexibility. That way when you cannot be flexible, they will know that it is imperative to hit the deadline, and they will kick into overdrive for you. By respecting your agency team to manage their resources, collaborating with them as partners, and treating them with empathy, you can continually expect positive performance.

If you take stock of how you are treating your agency and ensure that you extend its team the same empathy that you do for your own team, then they will work even harder to reward the trust you place in them and help you succeed, not just so your brand flourishes but so that you reach your goals as well.

* * *

By checking in on a regular basis to evaluate each other honestly and constructively, and by showing appreciation for each other as people, you are well on your way to a productive relationship with your ad agency, which can lead to success for your company as well as for your personal career.

In the final chapter of this book, I will briefly summarize the main points and take you behind the curtain on the agency side: how we at Fingerpaint select our clients, and what we do for them to ensure an incredibly positive relationship.

CHAPTER TEN

HOW FINGERPAINT SELECTS AND SERVES CLIENTS

Having run advertising agencies for the last twenty years, it strikes me how rarely people tell me that their agency is awesome. There's a huge underpinning of dissatisfaction with advertising agency partners across the board. When I meet a prospective client, they almost always say, "My agency's not strategic. They don't outthink me. I have the B team. I don't feel like I'm a priority. I always have to rewrite copy."

Whenever clients start working with a new agency, there's an initial euphoria, but over time, the bloom comes off the rose. When these relationships go south, it often happens because the culture inside the agency can be toxic for all the reasons that we've discussed in this book. As a result of a poor culture, account teams may get switched out due to high turnover, deadlines get missed, and clients start to feel that they're not getting great work and it's too expensive.

The stress of the daily work environment gets difficult. All of these factors lead to clients switching agencies every few years.

To avoid these pitfalls, all prospective purchasers of advertising should pay more attention to an agency's culture and the way the agency treats its human capital. When you find an agency with a culture of empathy and establish a relationship based on trust and caring, you can have mutual success for many years. That caring friendship between agency and client does wonders to make the work better, which in the long run means that you will have more consistency on the team, people will want to make the relationship work on both sides, and you'll have honest and transparent feedback.

At Fingerpaint, we've made culture a priority in the hopes of creating great, long-lasting client relationships with very strong work.

At Fingerpaint, we've made culture a priority in the hopes of creating great, long-lasting client relationships with very strong work. We've seen this bear fruit for us and our clients, and by following the lessons I've outlined in this book, you can similarly capitalize on the power of empathy and philanthropy to drive strong performance for your company. To sum up this book's main points in two sentences, you should do the following:

1. Select an agency with a culture of empathy and philanthropy.

2. After choosing an agency, continue to foster an empathetic culture.

SELECT AN AGENCY WITH A CULTURE OF EMPATHY AND PHILANTHROPY

To get the most out of your agency, which is a huge cost for your business and a huge influencer of your success, it's important to properly evaluate how that agency will be to work with day to day. As we've covered, a proper agency evaluation requires more than a proposal and a two-hour pitch.

If you take a deep look at the human side of the agency from the beginning and get to know the team that you will work with, you're more likely to find an agency that will treat you like a priority and build a strong collaborative partnership so that you won't have to rewrite copy or fix work that misses the mark creatively.

If an agency is a revolving door for clients and has poor ratings on Glassdoor, those are warning signs that you should give proper weight to—even if they've won a bunch of Clio Awards. There's a lot of great creative work being done in the industry, but fundamentally, the day-to-day grind of working with an ad agency will determine if your partnership succeeds or fails.

The way an agency treats its people is the best indicator of the way it will treat you. Leaders of agencies often wax poetic about their clients being number one: "We will walk through fire for you! No one is as important as you are, Mr. or Ms. Client!" But if they go back to the office and treat their staff poorly, then all of their grand words will ring hollow—it's nothing more than a sales pitch. If they do not treat their employees well, the employees will not treat you well. It's as simple as that. Over time, that will damage the work product.

At Fingerpaint, we put *our* people first and trust them to take great care of our clients. As a result, we've had clients for upward of eight years, which is pretty rare in our industry—especially for an agency that's only eleven years old at the time of this writing. We have a track record of keeping clients happy for a long time and of maintaining great relationships with clients even when their management teams shift.

AFTER CHOOSING AN AGENCY, CONTINUE TO FOSTER AN EMPATHETIC CULTURE

Once engaged with your agency, take the time to build a relationship based on mutual caring, and treat your agency as an extended part of your team. Day to day, lead your internal team with caring, and keep your finger on the pulse of your company's culture to ensure that it does not break down. Every quarter take a step back, measure your agency and your internal team from a human perspective, and allow your agency to measure your team as well, and you will be well on your way to consistently reaching your brand and career goals.

No matter your industry or which agency you choose, adhering to the lessons I've outlined in this book will help you drive success with your advertising partner. Next, I'll share how we select clients at Fingerpaint and what we do to ensure profitable relationships.

WHOM WE SERVE

We partner with marketing heads, managers, and procurement teams that value relationships with our people. Companies turn to us when they need a partner and not just a vendor to pump out tactics, when they want somebody to get in the foxhole with them and not let them down, and when they are looking for an agency that is more than a number on a spreadsheet, that can't be replaced by procurement with a swipe of the pen, because the brand teams would clamor to keep us.

Size of business isn't really a factor; we've had success with large, small, and midsize firms in the health-care, pharmaceutical, medical device, and health and wellness markets. The key to success for us and our clients is to find people who value the partnership between our two companies and put the patients they serve at the forefront.

We can provide the most value for those who need super agency firepower and are concerned that they'll get lost with a big agency. They come to us for projects ranging from launching new drugs for oncology or Alzheimer's to promoting specialized medical devices that treat brain injury all the way to marketing nutraceuticals focused on the consumer market.

Our bread and butter is helping companies that spend anywhere from half a million dollars up to $10 million per year on a health-care product or brand, who are looking for a strategic partner to shape the market with them—not an order taker to simply deliver tactics—and who wish to find a partner to build a profitable and caring relationship with.

HOW WE SELECT CLIENTS

Of course, we take our own advice about building relationships with you based on caring; when we pitch for new business, we invite you to spend time at our agency to get to know if it's a good fit. We take the time to get to know you up front when we sign on to work together, and we commit to going above and beyond in our work, respecting and valuing your team as people and continually measuring success. That's the recipe we've followed to develop long, fruitful relationships with clients in the past, and it's our road map for the future.

We don't accept any and every client that wants to work with us. Before agreeing to work for a client, we make sure that their product has a place in the market and that it's not just a money grab. We don't take on copycat drugs that do the same thing as existing products but at a higher price. We look for brands that will truly make a difference in the health community.

Obviously, there are varying degrees of the positive impact of each product. Some of our clients have revolutionary products that will help many people, and others may help only a small percentage of a patient population, but we always look for clients that we feel will better society. Our commitment to do good in the world extends beyond our focus on philanthropy; we choose clients that have good reputations, that are caring, and that put patients first.

As I'm sure you can tell from reading this book, we value our culture immensely, so we do not take clients that will treat our staff poorly or not value them as people. We look for people who respect us and our work, just like they expect us to respect theirs. As a result, we forge long-term relationships with those we work with, many of whom bring us along throughout the journey of their careers because they know we will do right by them and their brands.

Our best and happiest clients are the ones that take advantage of our strategic and creative firepower and let us work with them as a partner to shape and move markets. Because of our strategic acumen, it's not healthy for us to go into a relationship with a client who sees us as a supplier to take orders and crank stuff out. They don't need us—they can get that from a cheaper agency down the street—and we need to be able to provide more to ensure our client's success. When clients value us as partners, then we can bring an immense value to them through all of our strategic and tactical prowess.

WHAT OUR CLIENTS BENEFIT FROM

When you choose to work with Fingerpaint, you should expect our work to be strategically on the money and creatively disrupting and inspiring. We have a three-question creative standard that all 350-plus of our Fingerpainters live by:

1. Is what I'm doing paint by number?

2. Can I see the difference this will make?

3. Is it worth my signature?

We recruit the best people in the industry because of our culture and then empower them to do their best work by removing the traditional stress points ad agency workers deal with, such as fear of layoffs, health-care expenses, and so on. Unencumbered from those concerns, they can focus wholly on ensuring that everything we produce meets our three-question quality standard.

You should expect that our recommendations are sound, that we're fiscally responsible with your budget, that we're ethical, and that we'll do right by you and your patients. We're not in this business just to make money. We believe in making the world a better place through better health care, and that passion and enthusiasm rings true in our work. You should expect kind, smart, empathetic people whom you'll be proud to work with side by side.

We do the large majority of the above work in house. The major things we outsource are photographers, directors for commercials, and media buying. Typically, we manage the vendors for those services as well to make sure that everything is aligned strategically and creatively. Transparency is important to us, so when we create estimates and invoices, we detail which costs come from outside vendors, and unlike some agencies, we *never* mark up that work.

CORE COMPETENCIES AND CAPABILITIES

The bulk of our work is in the health-care space that is famous for the oath, "Do no harm." We take that responsibility to heart and have five core principles to ensure that we do right by our employees, our customers, and our communities.

OUR FIVE CORE PRINCIPLES

1. **We put people first:** You've heard what I have to say about this many times throughout this book. By treating our people like family instead of simply employees, we've hard wired putting people first into our DNA, which means that our clients can expect the same high level of care that we show our employees.

2. **We're independent by design:** Being free from the holding company machine lets us respond to your needs and not to a spreadsheet. So while many agencies call themselves "full service," we provide something better: "right service." We have the broad capabilities of a large network agency, but unlike holding company agencies, we don't need to "sell" certain services or work only with companies within a network. Our independence means we can take an honest look at your challenges and recommend what makes sense for you. We also can pull in experts when needed—we'll never say we're the best bunch for a task if we aren't. Fortunately, we love to collaborate, and we have great resources to tap into to meet your market challenge.

3. **We invest in our clients:** When we're with you, we're all in. We commit nonbillable hours to your brand as part of our dedication to your goals, and you get a constant stream of ideas and innovations to continually stay ahead of your competition.

4. **We create outside the lines:** Your customers demand more than just the same old fluff that they are used to seeing, so we employ marketing innovations such as brand journalism, information design, and interactive film to keep your brand making headlines.

5. **We don't just build brands; we activate them:** Marketing is no longer as simple as "if you build it, they will come." Your brand has to reach out onto mobile channels, connecting your customers where they live with the content they've been waiting for.

We live these five principles to ensure that we are accountable to the sales goals of your company. We motivate and excite your internal stakeholders, such as your sales force, medical science liaisons, managed care groups, and training departments. When you work with Fingerpaint, you sign up for good, ethical, hard-working, honest partners. That's who we are and what our clients benefit from.

If this sounds like something you're looking for, feel free to reach out and get to know us at Fingerpaint.

GRATITUDE TO MY WONDERFUL TEAM

I've worked as a marketing director, and I've run ad agencies for twenty-plus years. I still don't know how to make an ad, but I have learned how to put the best possible team together to provide brands great success and give the awesome people who make it happen a great place to work.

I treat my job like a general manager of a sports team; I'm never going to crush a home run or throw down a dunk, but I find people who are great at what they do and make sure that I give them everything they need as people and as coworkers to do the best work.

In these pages, I've shared my perspective gained from being on both sides of the marketing department and advertising agency relationship so that you can learn from my experience to find success.

Culture is the number-one factor I've seen for agencies that have succeeded in this business with happy clients. Agencies full of empathy and honesty that give back to the community generally do well. When I've seen agencies fail, it's usually because they forgot how important their people were; they became too focused on money and forgot that their business is their people.

When I come into work each morning and see the great people at Fingerpaint caring for each other, making great work, and bettering their communities, I feel a tremendous sense of loyalty and gratitude to the people who have given so much of their time to me over the years and have stayed with me for so long.

I really feel like a lucky son of a gun.

My philosophy for driving performance is built around an undying appreciation for the people who work with me and how fundamentally good they are to their cores. So thank you to my amazing staff for making Fingerpaint a great place to work each and every day.

ACKNOWLEDGMENTS

I want to thank all of the wonderful people who have worked with me over the years. Your hard work, laughter, positive attitudes, and friendships have helped us create some amazing health and wellness agencies, while helping so many patients around the globe.

To my wonderful family: my wife, Lisa, and my children Emily, Nick, and Grace. Thank you for all of your understanding and support when I worked late, traveled, and brought home stress. You have always been the brightest part of my life, and no man could ever ask for a stronger and more loving family in their corner. I am living the dream.

And to Ed Little, who gave me the courage, advice, love, and support to start my first health and wellness company when I was just thirty years old.

ABOUT THE AUTHOR

ED MITZEN has built health and wellness marketing firms from the ground up—not once, not twice, but three times, each more successful than the last. His first two ventures, CHS and Palio Communications, grew to $5 million and $25 million in revenue, respectively.

Ed founded Fingerpaint, an independent advertising agency, in Saratoga Springs, New York, in 2008. Ed's vision of putting employees first and giving back to others as frequently as possible is the bedrock of Fingerpaint's culture. From humble beginnings operating with card tables as desks, Fingerpaint has risen on the back of its people-first culture to employ more than 350 people in four locations across the United States, grossing $60 million in revenue in 2019.

Fingerpaint has been included on the "Inc. 5000" list of fastest-growing companies for seven straight years and garnered multiple agency of the year nominations and wins from MM&M, Med Ad News, and PM360. Ed was named Industry Person of the Year by *Med Ad News* in 2016 and a top boss by *Digiday* in 2017. He is a two-time nominee by Ernst & Young for the New York State Entrepreneur of the Year.

A Syracuse University alum with an MBA from the University of Rochester, Ed serves on the board of Syracuse's College of Arts and Sciences. He has also served on nearly a dozen charity and non-profit boards over the years.

You can find Ed's writing about entrepreneurship, empathetic leadership, and business in *Fortune*, *Forbes*, *HuffPost*, and the *Wall Street Journal*, among others.

Above all, Ed is most proud of being able to give back to his employees and partners and serving his community.